Praise for
I Love Disney's Magic Kingdom

"Danielle Kelly, affectionately known as The Dapper Danielle, has created an enchanting masterpiece with her book about Walt Disney's Magic Kingdom. Her passion shines through as she shares the stories of the ideas and incredible people who brought this dreamland to life. Her book is a treasure trove for anyone who loves Disney."

—**GWENDOLYN ROGERS**, owner and president of The Cake Bake Shop at Disney's BoardWalk Resort in Walt Disney World, Carmel City Center, and Broad Ripple Village

"*I Love Disney's Magic Kingdom* is a smart, insightful, and accessible exploration of the most magical place on Earth. Danielle's passionate storytelling and deep appreciation for the history of this iconic destination are pixie dusted from cover to cover. Whether you're a lifelong Disney lover or researching for your first trip to the Walt Disney World Resort, this book has something for you."

—**DANNY JORDAN**, award-winning author and TV producer of *Extreme Makeover: Home Edition*

"This isn't just a travel guide. It's a passport to the gifts of imagination, filled with stories and secrets—and sprinkled with pixie dust and confectionery delights! From Walt's inspirations to enchanting tales behind the attractions, Danielle brings the park to life in a way that only her love for all things Disney— and her experience as a Cast Member—can bring."

—**SANTA J CLAUS**, content creator and lover of all things magical (and churros and Dole Whips!)

I ♥ Disney's Magic Kingdom

100+ Surprising Facts, Magical Quizzes, Fan-Favorite Trivia, and More about Disney's Magic Kingdom!

DANIELLE KELLY @thedapperdanielle
with **IAN WILSON**

ADAMS MEDIA
NEW YORK AMSTERDAM/ANTWERP LONDON TORONTO
SYDNEY/MELBOURNE NEW DELHI

Adams Media
An Imprint of Simon & Schuster, LLC
100 Technology Center Drive
Stoughton, MA 02072

First Adams Media hardcover edition May 2025

ADAMS MEDIA and colophon are registered trademarks of Simon & Schuster, LLC.

Interior design by Sylvia McArdle
Interior maps and illustrations by Magic Around
Interior images © Adobe Stock

Manufactured in the United States of America

2 2025

Library of Congress Cataloging-in-Publication Data has been applied for.

ISBN 978-1-5072-2395-6
ISBN 978-1-5072-2396-3 (ebook)

CONTENTS

Map of Magic Kingdom

FRONTIERLAND

LIBERTY SQUARE

ADVENTURELAND

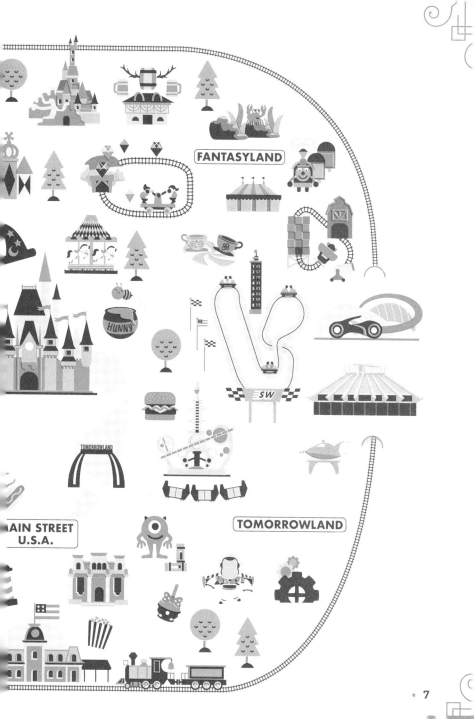

FANTASYLAND

HUNNY

1 43
2 57
3 79
4 81
5 83
6 85
7 89
8 92

SW

TOMORROWLAND

MAIN STREET
U.S.A.

TOMORROWLAND

Preface

The name on the cover of this book says Danielle Kelly, but I bet a lot of you know me as The Dapper Danielle from social media. My lifelong passion for the stories behind the magic of Disney gives me a unique, authentic perspective on Magic Kingdom . . . and I love sharing this endlessly entertaining information with the world. Before I became The Dapper Danielle and a source of Disney history, theme park information, and storytelling, I was a Disney kid. I grew up spending family vacations going to see "Uncle Mickey" at Disney. When I turned eighteen, I was inspired to begin working for the company.

I have always loved sharing my knowledge about Disney, so as a Cast Member for over nine-and-a-half years, I gravitated toward roles that allowed me to teach and entertain, such as Fairy Godmother at the Bibbidi Bobbidi Boutique and Merchandise Coordinator at Disney Springs. I developed a deep expertise in the individual storytelling that comes with each location and was also able to train other Cast Members.

My journey as a content creator began in early 2020 when COVID-19 shutdowns began. While I was able to visit with family during the lockdown, many of my fellow Cast Members were not as lucky, and they felt lonely, anxious, and afraid. In an attempt to ease the stress and uncertainty of the situation, I downloaded TikTok, primarily to connect with my friends and make goofy little videos to lift everyone's spirits.

One night during a Zoom party, a friend suggested that I should start making videos specifically about my expertise and authentic experiences as a Cast Member. I took that suggestion, and when Disney reopened, I started recording videos in my car late at night after my long shifts. In my videos, I shared guest questions and interactions from the day, fun tidbits about the parks, and positive words of encouragement. Slowly, these videos became informally called "Random Disney things in the middle of the night that you probably don't care about but I'm gonna tell you anyway." To my delight and surprise, people actually *did* care! As the weeks went on, more and more people from all around the world regularly checked out my late-night posts. Several hundred followers turned into several thousand, and then into hundreds of thousands.

I have always wanted to take all my "Random Disney Things" and turn them into a written guide—and that's what this book is. It's built from the hundreds of videos that I have posted on my social media, my personal experiences, and my love for finding out more about the most magical place on Earth. I am so excited to be able to tell you more about this place I love and point out my favorite spots along the way. Thanks for taking me with you!

—Danielle

Introduction

Exhilarating rides, creative storytelling, fascinating history, beloved characters, mouthwatering treats—Disney's Magic Kingdom has it all! Whether you've been to Magic Kingdom a dozen times, are currently at the park, or can't wait to go someday, *I Love Disney's Magic Kingdom* is a celebration of all the attractions, food, and behind-the-scenes trivia that make the park truly magical.

From the fairy-tale gleam of Cinderella Castle and out-of-this-world Space Mountain to the classic Casey's Corner hot dogs and cups of refreshing Dole Whip, Magic Kingdom is filled with one-of-a-kind experiences. Add a whole new layer of magic to your favorite park with hundreds of insightful tips, fun facts, and interactive quizzes that let you discover the park's rich history and hidden secrets.

To understand how incredible the park really is, you need to start at the beginning. First you'll dive into the remarkable story of the early days of Magic Kingdom—from the park's opening to the original rides and attractions that are still standing. Then you can use the map in the front of the book to follow along through each main area of Magic Kingdom, including Main Street U.S.A., Adventureland, Frontierland, Liberty Square, Fantasyland, and Tomorrowland. Each chapter is packed with insider information on key attractions (like rides, landmarks, and activities) and the top foods in that area (such as iconic menu items and popular restaurants). You'll learn entertaining details like:

* Why Main Street always smells so good
* Which dining location treats guests like royalty
* How fast you plummet down the big drop on Tiana's Bayou Adventure
* The architectural backstory of the plaza around the Pirates of the Caribbean ride
* Where to find specialty spring rolls
* The untold lore behind Big Thunder Mountain Railroad
* And more!

While you're exploring attractions and food, you'll have the chance to test your Disney knowledge with dozens of multiple choice, true-or-false, and matching quizzes. For example, do you know which famous actor applied to be a Jungle Cruise Skipper and did not get the job? Was it Josh Gad, Jim Gaffigan, or Terry Crews? (Turn to the back of the book to find out the answer!)

So, grab your Mickey ears, flip the page, and get ready to discover the magic behind the most magical place on Earth!

HOW TO USE THIS BOOK

Whether you are a first-time visitor making a once-in-a-lifetime trip to Magic Kingdom, an annual passholder making your hundredth trip, or a dreamer who hopes to visit someday, *I Love Disney's Magic Kingdom* has something valuable for you. Use it to get insider recommendations on food and attractions, learn little-known facts, and gain an even deeper appreciation of all Magic Kingdom has to offer.

This book starts with an overview and history of Magic Kingdom, and then is divided into chapters that focus on the different lands in Magic Kingdom. Each chapter features dozens of entries on:

Attractions, events, and special sites: From immersive rides to upbeat parades to world-class storytelling, these sections highlight the many unique places in Magic Kingdom. You'll also find directions on how to locate out-of-the-way or hard-to-find spots.

Food: Looking for a quick snack or a full sit-down dinner? You'll find options for both—and everything in between—in these scrumptious entries.

Quizzes: Test your knowledge of Walt Disney, Magic Kingdom itself, and the many amazing Disney films with multiple choice, matching, and true-or-false questions. (Check the Answers section in the back of the book to see if your answer is right!)

You can use the icons to quickly find specific entries (maybe you're looking for a place to eat in Tomorrowland), or you might choose to read the book from beginning to end. The entries for each chapter walk you through that land in order, site by site, and make you feel like you're at the park.

Along the way, you'll notice boxes that provide even more information:

★ **Extra Magic** gives you bonus details above and beyond what typical guidebooks share about attractions, park design, and more.

★ **Park Pointers** provide tips for Magic Kingdom visitors based on a lifetime of Disney park-going experience, such as the best time to visit a certain attraction. (Use these to make yourself the ultimate VIP tour guide for your group, #subtleflex.)

Ultimately, this book is yours to use however works best for you! Decide on the attractions you don't want to miss or history you want to keep an eye out for. Try to remember food that piques your interest or that obscure fact to wow your friends with later. Ask some trivia questions to pass the time in a queue line or on a road trip. Once you are back home, rereading this book will be sure to remind you of all your favorite spots.

Get ready to immerse yourself in an extraordinary world unlike anyplace else on Earth. Now let's get going on our trip to Magic Kingdom!

CHAPTER 1

Welcome to Magic Kingdom

As soon as you walk into Magic Kingdom, you can't help but sense the excitement and rich history that permeate every corner of the park. That's because each and every detail of the park's layout and design was fully thought out to make the guests' experience a truly unforgettable one. While the magical core of the park has stayed the same since opening day, it's taken more than fifty years for Magic Kingdom to grow into what it is today.

In this chapter, you'll go back to the very beginning and discover why Walt Disney had his eye on Florida for his new park—and just how much work was involved in making his dream come true. From what factors were involved in the search to just how long it took to build, you'll uncover all the moving parts behind the founding of Magic Kingdom. Then you'll witness the park's opening day and explore how Magic Kingdom looked back in the 1970s—from what celebrations took place to the twenty-five attractions that welcomed guests on that first day. Finally, you'll flash forward to today and dive deeper into the terms you need to know while familiarizing yourself with each section of the park. Now, let's start our journey where it all began—once upon a time . . .

WHERE THE MAGIC BEGAN

If you had visited the site of Walt Disney World in the 1950s, you would have only seen miles of cow fields and swampland under the hot Florida sun. There was little to suggest then that this area would eventually turn into one of the largest international tourist destinations in the world! But one person did imagine that this could happen: the man that started it all, Walt Disney.

Finding the Land

To understand the story of Magic Kingdom, we have to go back to the beginning—to the inception of Walt Disney World. Beginning in the early 1960s, Walt and his team of Imagineers were on the hunt to find the perfect location to set up a new park. Disneyland in California, which opened in 1955, had become a huge success, and Walt wanted to continue expanding the park. But there was a major problem—there wasn't enough room! Other companies, like hotels, restaurants, and gift shops, had quickly bought up property surrounding Disneyland to capitalize on the park's success. This limited Disney's ability to expand and add additional attractions and shows. There was simply no surrounding land that could be used to keep creating. Disneyland's success had become a boundary for growth.

To get around this issue of space in California, Walt wanted to create a second park and began hunting for the perfect location. But the selection wasn't easy—everything depended on three important factors:

1. First, the climate had to be similar to Southern California's. Walt wanted a place that he could keep open year-round without any seasonal closures. This meant a location that was relatively warm (and without snow)!
2. Second, the new location had to be big. Walt wanted as much land as possible to avoid facing the same issues he encountered in California.
3. Third, the land had to be affordable, since he was going to purchase such a large amount.

Walt soon realized Central Florida was one of the few places that checked all the boxes. In 1964, he began secretly buying up thousands of acres of land by using multiple fake aliases and dummy corporations to hide his intentions. After all, the price of the land would skyrocket if people discovered it was Disney who was looking to buy. The secret plan worked! It wasn't until the next year, on November 15, 1965, when Walt finally revealed his intentions to the public during a press event. For comparison, Disneyland property is currently about 500 acres, meaning you could fit a little over fifty-four Disneyland Parks and Resorts into the 27,440-acre Walt Disney World property! Walt said it himself on film talking about the "Florida Project" on October 27, 1966: "Here in Florida, we have something special we never enjoyed at Disneyland—the blessing of size. There is enough land here to hold all the ideas and plans we can possibly imagine." And imagine they did.

Breaking Ground on the Park

With the new land secured, The Walt Disney Company went to work transforming the fields and swamps into something magical. The first park to be created in Walt Disney's Florida Project was Magic Kingdom, with construction beginning in April 1969. In just eighteen months, Magic Kingdom, two resorts, one campground, and a large parking lot with a transportation hub were built. But it wasn't always smooth sailing—one of the biggest challenges was the surrounding swamp and wetlands regions.

On top of all the other construction that was going on, crews had to create more than 50 miles of levees and canals across the property to maintain water levels, help with drainage, and avoid contaminating the local water supply. The finishing touch was the massive Seven Seas Lagoon located just outside the gates of Magic Kingdom. The lagoon can comfortably hold the entirety of Magic Kingdom inside, or the equivalent of 127 football fields. One of the main reasons for creating the lagoon was to get soil to build the second floor of Magic Kingdom with the utilidors (short for "utility corridors") incorporated. However, the lagoon also helped create an immersive experience by forcing you to leave your vehicle and take a new form of transportation to a magical place (something that couldn't be done in Disneyland). In total, the project cost the Disney company $400 million in 1971, which comes out to the equivalent of $3.1 billion today after adjusting for inflation!

However, while the company was on the brink of a new, exciting future, it was also grieving the loss of its leader, Walt Disney. Sadly, Walt died from lung cancer just one year after Disney officially announced its plans for a new park. Although Walt didn't live to see his dream come to life, his brother Roy fiercely protected the original vision of the park at every turn. In a touching tribute, Roy chose to name the park in a way that honored his brother's legacy—calling it *Walt* Disney World.

THE CURTAIN RISES ON MAGIC KINGDOM

Magic Kingdom technically opened its gates on October 1, 1971, but the official grand opening of the park wouldn't take place until October 23. This gap was intentionally created to avoid another "Black Sunday." This is what the Disney workers called the 1955 Disneyland opening, which was riddled with overcrowding and technical issues. By using a soft opening over a few weeks, a team of 5,000 Cast Members had the time to fix minor issues and to reduce opening day crowds. The plan worked!

A One-of-a-Kind Opening Day

The opening day celebration was massive! The party lasted for three days and was star-studded, with guests like comedian Bob Hope, country music singer Glen Campbell, comic actor Buddy Hackett, and composer Meredith Wilson. One of the most memorable moments was Julie Andrews singing Disney classics like "It's a Small World." And to finish it all off, composer Meredith Wilson (creator of the musical *The Music Man*) led a grand band—which was almost three times the size of the largest American collegiate marching band—down Main Street to the tune of "Seventy-Six Trombones." As they paraded down the street, a mass choir, trumpet heralds, and a symphonic orchestra were waiting in front of Cinderella Castle to join them in a powerful performance of "When You Wish Upon a Star."

On the last day of the celebration, Roy Disney gave a dedication speech, honoring his late brother and stated a hope for the park: "May Walt Disney World bring joy and inspiration and new knowledge to all who come to this happy place." A few days later, the celebration aired on NBC, bringing the magic of Disney to homes across the nation. What a magical opening ceremony!

The Original Attractions

Did you know there were only twenty-five attractions available at Magic Kingdom during opening day? Visitors on that day could purchase a ticket book for $5.75, which included your admission into the park, your transportation ticket, and your attraction tickets. With your transportation ticket, you could use any and all modes of travel from the Transportation and Ticketing Center and Magic Kingdom's front gate as many times as you'd like. The options included parking lot trams, boats, and the monorail.

But the attraction tickets only let you choose one attraction per category. "E" tickets included some of the most technologically advanced and in-demand attractions, like Jungle Cruise and Haunted Mansion, while "A" tickets included some of the less thrilling attractions, like Cinderella's Golden Carrousel and Main Street Vehicles. That's only five attractions total—an impossible decision! Which ones would you choose?

"E" Attractions
★ "it's a small world"
★ 20,000 Leagues Under the Sea: Submarine Voyage
★ The Mickey Mouse Revue
★ Jungle Cruise
★ Tropical Serenade
★ Haunted Mansion

"D" Attractions
★ Walt Disney World Railroad
★ Skyway to Fantasyland and Tomorrowland
★ Flight to the Moon
★ Country Bear Jamboree
★ The Hall of Presidents
★ Admiral Joe Fowler Riverboat

"C" Attractions
★ Grand Prix Raceway
★ Dumbo the Flying Elephant
★ Peter Pan's Flight
★ Snow White's Adventures
★ Mr. Toad's Wild Ride
★ Mad Tea Party
★ Davy Crockett's Explorer Canoes

"B" Attractions
★ Main Street Cinema
★ Frontierland Shootin' Gallery

- ★ Mike Fink Keel Boats
- ★ Swiss Family Treehouse

"A" Attractions
- ★ Main Street Vehicles
- ★ Cinderella's Golden Carrousel

You may have spotted some familiar names on these lists—while a few of the opening day attractions are still operating, many have been renamed or replaced. Plus, the total number of attractions in the park has doubled since 1971! As you can see, Disney World has come a long way since that opening day.

BEHIND THE CURTAIN

Disney World has soared into everything Walt imagined and more. But it takes a lot of work (and people) to make the magic happen! Enter the Cast Members, or Disney employees. Today, more than 80,000 Cast Members work across Disney World properties, including all parks, hotels, and sites, making it one of the largest single-site employers in the United States. The term "Cast Member" originated with Walt himself when describing park operations. The Disney company has its roots in show business, and Disney treated the park like a giant movie set. Every Cast Member has an essential role in helping the magic of the stage come to life. All employees are referred to as Cast Members regardless of whether they are an hourly employee, a manager, or a designer. While we're talking about Cast Members, here are some more essential park operations terms referenced in this book:

- ★ **Role:** A role is a Cast Member's specific job or title. Because so many Cast Members play different roles (or do the same role in multiple parks in one day), there isn't an exact number of how many Cast Members are working in Magic Kingdom at any given time!

- ★ **Costumes:** Instead of employee uniforms, Cast Members wear costumes. These costumes are typically in-theme with the land or area where the Cast Members work. For example, Disney Cast Members in Frontierland don yellow and brown costumes that are western themed, while Tomorrowland Cast Members wear costumes that are blue and purple and project a futuristic theme. Of course, individual attractions can also have their own costumes that fit within the general theme of the area (Haunted Mansion, for example). Disney has recently been making strides to create its Cast Members' costumes out of recycled material.

- ★ **Onstage and Backstage:** In the same sense that Cast Members are actors playing a large role in how the park operates, the park itself is a giant stage. Disney refers to areas with guests around as "onstage," while areas like office buildings, break rooms, and other places that do not typically have guests are considered "backstage."

A PEEK BACKSTAGE

Now that you know the lingo, let's talk about a very specific backstage location. Did you know that under Main Street (and elsewhere in the park) are utility tunnels used by Cast Members? These tunnels are called utilidors, short for "utility corridors," and allow Cast Members to move from one end of the park to the other without "breaking show." Legend goes that one day when Walt Disney was walking around Disneyland, he spotted a Cast Member walking into work through Tomorrowland wearing his Frontierland costume. Disney thought that sights like these would detract from the overall guest experience. After all, why would a cowboy be walking around the future?

But again, Disneyland faced limitations. The park was already built with no easy way of adding a tunnel system underneath. With the creation of Magic Kingdom from the ground up, engineers were able to incorporate utilidors, which have played a large role in how the park operates. You may be imagining tight and narrow passageways, but the majority are wide enough for golf carts and forklifts to pass through without blocking Cast Members!

The main path goes in a circle around the park with walkways to different areas like break rooms, offices, training rooms, electrical rooms, waste management, emergency services, and entertainment practice rooms. With so many moving parts, this area is definitely not safe for the average guest. If you are interested in seeing the utilidors, you can get a glimpse into park operations as part of the Keys to the Kingdom tour in Magic Kingdom. This tour is a five-hour walking tour that goes in-depth into the story of Magic Kingdom and takes you into a portion of the utilidors to get a peek behind the curtain.

A WALK IN THE PARK

You've learned about how Magic Kingdom came to be and some hidden secrets that make everything run smoothly. First let's talk about the way Magic Kingdom is set up. Then we'll dive into the six main sections of the park (Main Street U.S.A., Adventureland, Frontierland, Liberty Square, Fantasyland, and Tomorrowland). Along the way, you'll learn about some unique features, area highlights, and what to expect in each chapter.

The Hub

Did you know that the center of Magic Kingdom is shaped like a wheel with spokes leading to the different lands? This was done intentionally to help guests navigate the park. The location of the center of the park (the area in front of Cinderella Castle and around the *Partners* statue) is nicknamed the "Hub."

Now, it's time to take a deeper look at each land that makes up Magic Kingdom!

Main Street U.S.A.

Main Street U.S.A. is designed to resemble an 1880s–1910s main street from a small turn-of-the-century town on the coast of the northeastern United States. This is the main area for souvenir shopping and delicious treats. Here you might run into the world-famous Dapper Dans or enjoy a performance by the Casey's Corner pianist tickling the ivories. While there aren't any rides on Main Street, the area more than makes up for it with immersive storytelling and streetmosphere galore! There is a candy store, sit-down Italian dining, and some other fun treats that you can find out about in Chapter 2.

Extra Magic

★

Disney has been setting the standard in theme park entertainment for years and has even created some of its own terms and phrases for such entertainment—that's where "streetmosphere" comes in. Disney coined the term "streetmosphere" to describe the entertainment and performers that appear in and around walkways to personally interact with guests. A key element of streetmosphere is that the performers are time period specific or closely connected to the theme of the area of the park.

Left or Right?

Now to address one of the most pressing questions that faces Magic Kingdom visitors: Once you enter Magic Kingdom and pass through Main Street U.S.A., do you turn left or right? Right will take you straight into Tomorrowland, while left will bring you into Adventureland (hypothetically, you could also begin by going straight through Cinderella Castle and starting in Fantasyland, but that choice is impractical for those that want to see all the park). There are a few reasons you should listen to this Disney expert and turn left!

1. You'll be going in the opposite direction of traffic since most guests turn right.
2. Magic Kingdom's design is oriented to the points of a compass. If you are standing at the *Partners* statue of Walt and Mickey in the Hub, facing Cinderella Castle to the north, Tomorrowland is east, Main Street is south, and Adventureland is west. This is critical for the blazing Florida sun. By starting in Adventureland at the beginning of the day, the rising sun will be at your back. By the time you are moving to Tomorrowland at the end of the day, the sun will have moved and now be setting at your back. This reduces the strain on your eyes, and you'll be more comfortable throughout the day.
3. Going to the left is how this book is organized, so make things easier on yourself and follow its lead!

As Main Street is the only way in and out of the park, you will pass through it at least twice during your visit. In a way, it is the opening and closing credits of your day in the park!

Adventureland

Adventureland transports you to the wild world of explorers, exotic lands, and the search for treasure. Here you'll find goofy Jungle Cruise Skippers, singing birds, pineapple delights, and bloodthirsty pirates. This land has some of the best-hidden details in the decor and even on the walkways. While venturing past The Magic Carpets of Aladdin and Agrabah Bazaar, look around on the ground and you may see necklaces, coins, mosaic tiles, and gems. Adventure is so close you can almost taste it . . . or drink it! As you pass by the entrance of Jungle Cruise, there is an unusual water fountain surrounded by crates. Pay attention to the labels written on the crates—you might just be drinking water from a box containing piranhas! Little details like this are what make Adventureland truly unique.

Park Pointer

★

If you're planning on (or are currently) visiting the park, don't forget to download the My Disney Experience app. The app helps with everything: wait times for attractions, ride closure notifications, mobile orders for food, mobile checkout for merchandise, dining reservations, GPS walking directions through the park, a map of the bathrooms, and everything in between!

Frontierland

Frontierland continues with the same sense of adventure as you are transported to the great American Southwest. Are you brave enough to hop aboard an out-of-control mine train traveling through mine shafts that are caving in? What about taking a 52-foot plunge down into the bayou with a bunch of singing critters? If you can't bear the thought of either of these options, head over to the middle of Frontierland, where a band of grizzly characters are putting on a show. Frontierland is one land that has experienced many changes over the years, but that only makes it more true to the ever-changing spirit of the frontier that inspired it. While new things are always coming to Frontierland, one thing remains a constant: an appreciation of the past. Frontierland honors the stories and legends that helped pioneer America.

Liberty Square

Liberty Square transports you from the Southwest frontier to the colonial days of the northeastern United States. Liberty Square pays homage to America's history with food and entertainment. Walt Disney was a big fan of American history, so this land was placed here in honor of Walt and is the only land in a Disney park around the world dedicated to this theme. You can read more about why this is in Chapter 4! As a bonus—just like in so many American towns—there's a house on the hill that's rumored to be haunted.

Fantasyland

Fantasyland is the gateway into imagination! This is the land of princesses, castles, flying elephants, and spinning teacups. While walking around the land you may run into Peter Pan as he plays hide-and-seek with visitors. If you're lucky (or unlucky, depending on your view), you may hear Anastasia and Drizzela practicing one of their singing lessons or meeting guests behind the castle. Fantasyland truly is a magical place that carries a nearly constant sense of that classic "Disney feeling." Walt Disney said it best on July 17, 1955: "Fantasyland is dedicated to the young and the young in heart, to those that believe that when you wish upon a star, your dreams do come true."

Tomorrowland

Tomorrowland transports you to infinity and beyond, with an imagining of what the world could be. Here aliens play keyboard for burger joints, monsters imagine a world powered by laughs, and whizzing through the cosmos is just another morning commute. While many of the attractions look forward to the world of tomorrow, Tomorrowland also honors the past. Attractions like Walt Disney's Carousel of Progress take us on a journey through history to discover what could lie ahead. Walt's original vision for the land was to showcase a place where science and new ideas could lead the next generation and bring hope for a peaceful and unified world.

MAKING MAGICAL MEMORIES

Magic Kingdom is the most visited theme park in the entire world! Over 18 million people visit Magic Kingdom every year, with around 50,000 people walking through the gates each day! So, what brings people to Magic Kingdom? Is it the Cast Members? Is it the food? Is it the rides? The answer is yes, but none of those are the main reason why people come. The reason is because Magic Kingdom plucks us from our reality, takes us on adventures, transports us to the land of make believe, and gives us hope for a "great, big beautiful tomorrow, shining at the end of every day." Guests come here to make memories with their families every single day, which really is the most powerful magic of all.

Lower your lap bar and keep your hands and feet inside the ride at all times as you embark on your adventure through each land in Magic Kingdom!

CHAPTER 2

Main Street U.S.A.

Entering Magic Kingdom is truly captivating—you're immediately transported back in time to a small American town that feels inviting and comforting. Welcome to Main Street U.S.A.! The design of Main Street was inspired by the small towns that could be found along the northeastern coast of the United States during the late 1800s and early 1900s, but the area also borrows inspiration from Fort Collins, Colorado, and Walt Disney's boyhood home of Marceline, Missouri.

This chapter is dedicated to the unique features, delicious foods, can't-miss attractions, and hidden gems of Main Street. Whether it's your first time walking down Main Street or your hundredth time, there are always new details to be discovered. Some of them might just become your favorite features of Magic Kingdom! Let's take a closer look at this charming area and discover the magic within!

⚙ IMMERSE YOURSELF IN A MOVIE SET

Did you know that Main Street is basically a movie set? This section of the park features some of the same design elements that the Disney production companies use when creating sets for live-action movies! The entire area utilizes a construction technique borrowed from movie production called forced perspective, which changes the scale of buildings' facades as they get taller so that the higher levels of buildings are shorter and smaller than they would be in real life. This technique tricks our brains into believing that the buildings are the same size as actual buildings, leading to a more immersive experience.

As mentioned, Main Street U.S.A. is based on the look of Fort Collins, Colorado, and Walt Disney's boyhood home of Marceline, Missouri. One specific *fictional* town that was also incorporated into the storytelling of Main Street is Beulah, Maine, from the 1963 Disney movie *Summer Magic*, starring Hayley Mills and Burl Ives. There are multiple references to the movie *Summer Magic* hidden throughout Main Street, but two of them are pretty easy to find:

1. One is located under Main Street Train Station. To find the reference to *Summer Magic*, you need to walk behind the center stairs to the area with the train bulletin board. One of the schedules lists a stop at Beulah.
2. The second reference is located on the Emporium shop. Before you head down Main Street toward Cinderella Castle, turn to your left and look at the windows to the right of the corner entrance of the Emporium directly across from the confectionery. On the window to the right of the door, you will see that the proprietor

of Emporium is listed as "Osh" Popham. He is the postmaster, caretaker, and shopkeeper in the town of Beulah and was played by Burl Ives.

? WHY DOES MAIN STREET ALWAYS SMELL SO GOOD?

Disney Imagineering is famous for ensuring that everything you see or touch is part of an immersive experience. But what you smell is just as important, so Disney has a patented system to ensure that your sniffer gets in on the magic as well. This system was first patented by Disney in 1986 and pumps pleasing scents onto Main Street and other attractions around the parks. Fun fact: The smells on Main Street change with the seasons, ranging from sugary pastries to pumpkin spice and peppermint.

True or False: Disney's patented aromatic system is called a Smellitizer.

WHERE ARE THOSE TRAINS GOING, ANYWAY?

It wouldn't be Disney if even the smallest-seeming details weren't meaningful Easter eggs! For a fun peek at some Disney history, check out the train bulletin board under the train station as you walk into the park. Some of the stops have meaningful Disney connections:

★ Chicago: where Walt Disney was born.
★ Marceline: where Walt Disney spent his childhood years from 1906–1911.

- ★ Kansas City: where Walt Disney created his first cartoon studio, called Laugh-O-gram Films.
- ★ Fort Wilderness: a reference to the campground and one of the three resorts that opened in Walt Disney World in 1971.
- ★ Medfield: a fictional place where many of Disney's live-action films in the late 1960s and 1970s took place—most notably *The Absent-Minded Professor* (1961), where Professor Brainard taught at Medfield College.
- ★ Rutledge: the sports rival town of Medfield.
- ★ Rainbow Caverns: a place in Nature's Wonderland; an extinct attraction that ran from 1956–1959 in Disneyland's Frontierland.
- ★ Grizzly Bear Flats: a reference to Grizzly Flats Railroad, which was a full-sized backyard railroad that was owned by Disney animator Ward Kimball. This railroad also influenced the design of Disneyland Railroad.

THE MOST MAGICAL MEET AND GREET ON MAIN STREET

Step back from the hustle and bustle of Main Street and visit Town Square Theater to smile and say, "Cheese!" with the big cheese himself: Mickey Mouse! Town Square Theater is located on the right side of the street as you pass under the train station. Typically, this meet-and-greet location is reserved just for Mickey, but Minnie will join him for special occasions and around holiday events.

At this location, you are transported "backstage" of the theater to Mickey's dressing room, where he is ready to greet guests in his magician outfit. The queue and the dressing room itself are full of fun nods and Easter eggs to other magical characters. For example, the crystal ball on the top shelf of the dressing room is engraved "Leota Crystals. Model 1969," which is a reference to the disembodied ghost head of Madame Leota that resides in the séance room of Haunted Mansion, along with the opening year of the attraction in Disneyland. Keep your eyes open for more magical Easter eggs throughout this fun meet-and-greet location.

Park Pointer

★

Town Square Theater is also the home of the Disney PhotoPass counter at Magic Kingdom. Here, PhotoPass Cast Members can assist with printing or finding your photos. Ever gotten off a ride only to find that the ride photo is not appearing in your app? Make a note of the time you were getting on or off the attraction and then swing by the PhotoPass counter, where a Cast Member will be happy to help you find it.

❓ MICKEY'S FIRST WORDS

Everyone knows what Mickey looks like, but do you know what his first words in a film were? I'll give you a few hints. These words were spoken in his appearance in the 1929 cartoon short titled *The Karnival Kid*. Although Mickey made eight appearances in film prior to this short, he only made simple noises, like whistling, laughing, and crying. Contrary to popular belief, these first words were not voiced by

Walt Disney, although Walt would go on to perfect the high-pitched voice of Mickey in subsequent shorts. Instead, Mickey's first words were voiced by composer Carl W. Stalling.

What were Mickey's first words?

- **A.** "Oh, boy!"
- **B.** "Hiya, pal!"
- **C.** "Hot dogs! Hot dogs!"

Extra Magic

★

Located next to City Hall is Main Street's firehouse and home of "Engine 71" (a subtle nod to the year the park opened, 1971). This firehouse is also home to hundreds of patches from fire stations around the world donated by firefighters over the years. Can you find a patch from your hometown?

MAGICAL MUSIC

Over the years, certain parts of Disney's streetmosphere have changed, but one iconic group of entertainers remain on Main Street: The Dapper Dans! This barbershop quartet has been performing in Magic Kingdom since the opening day of Disney World in 1971 (though the group actually began in Disneyland in 1959). Barbershop quartets gained popularity in America around the 1900s, making this style of music a perfect addition to the idyllic setting of Main Street as a turn-of-the-century town center. The Dapper Dans perform seven days a week between the hours of around 9:00 a.m. and 3:30 p.m. You can find the exact times of their daily performances on the My Disney Experience app.

Extra Magic

★

The Dapper Dans don't perform the same old tunes every day. They sing a variety of songs, from American classics to Disney-specific tunes. As the seasons change, so will the Dans' set lists, outfits, and even jokes. During Mickey's Not-So-Scary Halloween Party, you might even get to see The Cadaver Dans. This "undead" version of the quartet sings eerie songs from some of your favorite Disney villains.

❓ REAL-LIFE MAIN STREET SERVICES

Like any small town in America, Main Street U.S.A. has provided a number of real public services to its "townspeople" (aka park guests) over the years. Thanks to these services, Main Street is both fun and functional! For example, from 1971–1997, Main Street featured a town bank that was operated by Sun Bank (later known as SunTrust).

While most of Main Street's services are no longer operational, which one is still functional—and features an authentic, turn-of-the-twentieth-century piece of equipment?

A. Firehouse

B. Mail service

C. Dry cleaners

RIDE DOWN MAIN STREET IN STYLE

Ever wanted to drive right down the middle of Main Street U.S.A.? Throughout the morning and midafternoon, you may be lucky enough to take a one-way trip down Main Street using a turn-of-the-twentieth-century-inspired car or bus. You can hop aboard one of these vehicles near Main Street Train Station or Town Square Theater and take a ride toward the front of Cinderella Castle. (These vehicles do not typically operate during inclement weather, and the schedule can change daily depending on the events happening within the park.)

One of the most impressive vehicles in the fleet is a double-decker omnibus. Did you know that this type of bus was originally created for use in EPCOT? It premiered in 1982 and served as a free mode of transportation around World Showcase Lagoon. In the late 1990s, Disney began to repurpose such buses as character floats or as traveling stages for bands and performers. Eventually many of the buses were sold or torn apart; however, one was reimagined and moved to Magic Kingdom because the design of the bus already matched the aesthetic of Main Street. The omnibus has since taken thousands of guests every year up and down Main Street. Some small details remain on the bus referencing its days in service at EPCOT. For example, look for the EPCOT logo hidden in the center of the steering wheel!

Extra Magic

★

Much of the design for Main Street U.S.A. was created by John DeCuir, an experienced production designer. He was responsible for many movie sets made famous on the big screen, including the iconic sets from the 1890s-themed New York City scenes in *Hello, Dolly!* (1969).

HAVE YOUR OWN *LADY AND THE TRAMP* MOMENT

It is a beautiful night . . . to find a hidden *Lady and the Tramp* reference, that is! One interesting aspect of Main Street U.S.A. is that very few Disney films are promoted in the area. This is because there are very few Disney movies that are set in America between 1880 and 1910.

One exception? Tony's Town Square Restaurant, inspired by the animated movie *Lady and the Tramp*. Though the movie was released in 1955, it takes place in 1909, making it an ideal fit for the time period of Main Street. The Disney Imagineers incorporated a nod to the romantic spaghetti scene in the film by placing Lady's and Tramp's paw prints in the sidewalk just outside Tony's Restaurant. To find the paw prints, look outside and to the left of the restaurant. You will see a covered porch with five arches in front. If you look on the ground in front of the central arch, you will see the paw prints on the sidewalk (this area is also stroller and wheelchair parking for the restaurant, so it is easier to find later in the evening).

 SPAGHETTI FOR TWO

Tony's Town Square Restaurant stands just past the entrance to Magic Kingdom as the first sit-down restaurant you will encounter. The restaurant is themed after the romantic spaghetti scene from the movie where the restaurant's owner, Tony, and employee Joe serve a candle-light dinner and some incredible pasta. In the movie, we don't get much of a glimpse of the inside of the restaurant since the scene takes place in the back alley. This restaurant transports us into what that restaurant may have looked like on the inside, complete with a fountain statue of the doggie sweethearts. Naturally, spaghetti and meatballs are always available on the menu, but there are many other fabulous dishes, such as Fried Mozzarella, Rigatoni alla Vodka, Tortellini and Italian Sausage al Forno, and the occasional seasonal offering. Don't forget to leave room for dessert!

CANDY AND COOKIES AND SNACKS, OH MY!

A trip down Main Street wouldn't be complete without a sweet treat. One of the best places to find one is at Main Street Confectionery. The confectionery is one of the first buildings to greet you as you enter the park—and its placement is connected to Walt Disney's childhood.

Walt's boyhood home of Marceline, Missouri, opened a confectionery shop in 1905, the year before Disney's family moved into town. The little shop was one of the first buildings that would have greeted you as you entered town from the south. Walt grew up passing that confectionery regularly and looking into the shop window with his buddies, probably licking their lips a bit as they peered at the caramel, chocolate, and taffy treats through the window. These memories stayed with Walt and heavily influenced the location of this candy shop.

❓ A CONFECTIONERY COMPETITION

Since there aren't a lot of Disney movies representing turn-of-the-twentieth-century America, the Disney Imagineers have created their own stories for the area. One example is the story of the Sweetest Spoon Showcase within Main Street Confectionery. The story revolves around the idea that Main Street Confectionery is where award-winning chefs and bakers from across the country are exhibiting their talents. Six characters were created with varying backgrounds, ethnicities, and cultures, all with their own signature items that won them the Sweetest Spoon Showcase. When you enter the confectionery, look for the pillar just inside the doors closest to the flagpole outside, which is where all the showcase winners' stories are written out. You can read all about Dr. Alsoomse Tabor's fruit leather and Toshi Hayakawa's rice cake, among several others.

Main Street Confectionery is currently sponsored by the Mars company. In the back of Kernel Kitchen are images referencing the history of the Mars company along with a black-and-white photo of a horse behind the counter. That horse's name inspired one of the company's most famous candy bars.

Which candy bar was named after the horse?

- **A.** Milky Way
- **B.** Snickers
- **C.** Twix

 POP IN FOR A TASTY SNACK

Hidden in the back of Main Street Confectionery, toward the right side of the store and up the ramp, is Kernel Kitchen. This corner of the confectionery allows a Cast Member to make you your own custom popcorn mix. This is one of the best snacks in Magic Kingdom! The process is broken down into three easy steps:

1. **Choose your base popcorn flavor.** A variety of flavors is available and changes out seasonally, but don't worry, classic buttered popcorn or caramel is typically available all year round.
2. **Choose your syrup.** You can add a drizzle of white, dark, or milk chocolate syrup.
3. **Choose your candy.** Do you want to add pretzels? M&M's? Maybe even Skittles? The choices are endless!

Can't decide what to create or don't want to wait in line for a custom mix? A small selection of specialty and seasonal mixes are available for mobile order on the My Disney Experience app and are mixed fresh within minutes.

❓ SHARING THE MAGIC

As you enter Main Street, you may see a PhotoPass photographer helping families take pictures next to a statue of a man sitting on a park bench casually chatting with Minnie Mouse. People will often pose for a picture near it, believing that the man in the statue is Walt Disney. The statue actually depicts Walt's brother Roy and is a tribute to his hard work to make Disney World come to life. While the Florida Project was Walt Disney's dream, it was Roy who brought the project to completion after Walt's passing in 1966. Roy became the Disney company's first CEO and would later give the Florida Project the official name of Walt Disney World in honor of his brother. The contributions Roy made to continue Walt's dreams and legacy were commemorated in 1999 with the installation of this bronze statue. It's called *Sharing the Magic*, and it was sculpted by Blaine Gibson.

There is one small detail in the statue that is important: Is Roy's hand above or below Minnie's hand?

 A WINDOW INTO DISNEY LEGENDS

Avid Disney fans will be very familiar with the windows above the store and restaurant facades of Main Street. Many of these higher windows have names of people and businesses written on them. The names feature people who played a significant role in the creation, development, and operation of Magic Kingdom and Disney World. The businesses listed next to the names are not real but are clever nods to what that person contributed.

For example, above the right side of the main confectionery entrance, on the second floor, you will see a series of five windows. The first window on the left reads: "General Joe's Building Permits." This window honors William E. ("Joe") Potter, a retired United States Army major general that Walt Disney personally hired in 1965 as vice president of Florida planning. Joe is considered the first official employee of Walt Disney World and oversaw nearly all the construction and infrastructure in Magic Kingdom, from the underground utilities to drainage canals. He was the "boots on the ground," communicating with local officials on behalf of the team still in California.

Joe passed away on December 5, 1988, and the next day, President of Walt Disney Attractions Dick Nunis told the *Orlando Sentinel*, "He was a man Walt Disney was very fond of. Without Joe Potter, there would be no Walt Disney World today." It is only fitting that his window is one of the first you see upon entering the park.

❓ NOT A REGULAR JOE

Speaking of General Joe Potter, his name appears somewhere else in Disney World.

Where else can you see Joe Potter mentioned?

A. Street sign on Main Street

B. Jungle Cruise life ring

C. Ferryboat on Seven Seas Lagoon

Extra Magic

★

Did you know that you can listen in on a singing lesson or a dance class on Main Street? Nestled between Uptown Jewelers and Crystal Arts is a little seating alcove, perfect for enjoying a coffee from Main Street Bakery or a sweet treat from Main Street Confectionery. Above this seating area on the second floor of the Crystal Arts building are windows that read, "Voice & Singing— Private Lessons" and "Music & Dance Lessons—Ballet, Tap & Waltz." From these windows, you may hear a music teacher giving vocal instruction, someone practicing their scales, or a dance instructor giving directions for a tap number. Take a moment to sit and listen carefully to see who is taking a lesson that day.

🍴 WE ALL SCREAM FOR ICE CREAM

What's one of the first things you think of when it comes to theme park sweets? Ice cream! Plaza Ice Cream Parlor is the place to go for an ice cream on Main Street. Located on the corner across from Casey's, it serves a multitude of ice cream flavors and is known for seasonal offerings. One of the most popular options at Plaza Ice Cream is the Mickey Kitchen Sink Sundae, a shareable ice cream treat that comes in a souvenir cup. The cup is shaped like a sink version of Mickey's shorts, complete with a black faucet and Mickey gloves for knobs. The contents of the sundae itself are mostly up to you. Choose two of your favorite ice cream flavors and whether you would like hot fudge or caramel on top. The sundae is then topped with whipped cream and two cherries. It's the perfect indulgence and souvenir, since you can reuse the bowl at home. Make your own sundaes in it or use it as a cereal bowl or even as a new pot for your succulents.

🍴 COMFORT FOOD WITH A CASTLE VIEW

Hidden on the edge of Main Street, just before entering Tomorrowland Terrace Restaurant, is a little eatery called The Plaza Restaurant. You might be thinking that the name of the restaurant is suspiciously similar to the ice cream parlor next door. That's because they were connected once upon a time. When the two spaces opened in 1971, what's now the restaurant was the seating area of the ice cream parlor. This connection proved to be short-lived, however, and the two spaces were divided in 1977, making The Plaza one of the smallest sit-down restaurants on the property, with a max capacity of fewer than eighty guests.

The restaurant makes up for its small space with its elegant art nouveau style. This style peaked during the turn of the twentieth century, making it well suited for a Main Street U.S.A. restaurant, and the nouveau swirls and large mirrors adorning every wall help this tiny gem feel just a little larger. While this restaurant may not be ideal for large parties, guests who visit will be greeted by a small menu featuring some "soda shop" classics like loaded fries, onion rings, and milkshakes. If you're searching for something a little less fried, the Triple Decker Turkey Club Sandwich and Pot Roast Stack are great options. This restaurant is the perfect place to sit and relax during the heat of the day, with some seats offering views of the Hub and Cinderella Castle.

 TOO MUCH MAGIC?

When Magic Kingdom opened, Disney did a good job of avoiding chaos by spreading out its opening celebration across multiple days. The same can't be said for one of its first holiday celebrations, though. On this holiday, Disney World reached max capacity in the park and the parking lot. More than 5,000 cars were turned away by 2:00 p.m., and the state had to close the access ramps off of I-4, which led to a backup of 20–30 miles in both directions on the four-lane interstate. (While Disney manages floods of crowds around the holidays better now, the festive seasons still bring lots of guests and delays, so plan accordingly.)

Which holiday celebration was the first to make Disney World reach max capacity?

- **A.** Thanksgiving/Black Friday
- **B.** Fourth of July
- **C.** Christmas
- **D.** Halloween

THE WORLD-CLASS ARTISTRY OF THE ARRIBAS BROTHERS

As you walk down Main Street, you might have started peeking at the window displays along the street. If you look into the Crystal Arts store, you can see beautiful pieces of art made of glass and crystal. This little store is one of the oldest "third-party" contracts in the history of the Disney parks. It all started with the Arribas brothers and Walt Disney.

In the early 1960s, two brothers from La Coruña, Spain, were chosen by the Spanish Cultural Ministry to represent the culture of Spain in the 1964 World's Fair, which took place in New York City. The brothers were recognized as masters of glassblowing and cutting, which was an art passed down in their family for generations. During their time at the World's Fair, Walt Disney became fascinated by their work—so much so that Walt offered them a spot to open their first store inside Disneyland. They accepted his offer, and with a third brother opened their Disneyland store in 1967 and their Magic Kingdom location in 1971. The rest is history, and now there are Arribas Brothers stores in every Disney Park around the world, with twenty-four locations and four generations of master artisans creating stunning pieces of glass and crystal art—with a magical Disney touch, of course.

Inside the Crystal Arts store in Magic Kingdom, you can see artists creating one-of-a-kind pieces during the day. One special thing about the Arribas Brothers store in Magic Kingdom is that in the back of the shop is a glassblowing furnace, where an artist will create large pieces to be sold in the store. During the fall season you can witness a demonstration on how large glass pumpkins are made. Or stop by in the winter months to see how glass ornaments are blown. The demonstration times are not always on a regular schedule, so check in with a Cast Member to see when you might be able to watch an artist at work.

❓ THE BACKSTORY OF A MAIN STREET STAPLE

Treb Heining is the creator of the globe-style Mickey balloon that is sold on Main Street today. Treb started as a Cast Member in Disneyland in charge of selling balloons on Main Street. His fascination with balloons grew, until he eventually left Disney and started his own balloon business. Through a connection, he designed the birthday decorations for a party for Cher's son, Elijah Blue Allman. One of the decor pieces was a balloon arch, which is credited as the first-ever balloon arch in history!

He then became the balloon man of Hollywood, designing displays for grand opening events, television programs, and even the opening ceremonies for the Olympics. Twenty-five years after Treb left Disney, he was enlisted by Disney to create a new balloon, and the result was the famous "glasshouse" balloon that places a latex Mickey-shaped balloon inside a clear balloon. The updated Mickey balloon was introduced in 1998 as has been a top seller ever since.

What do the glasshouse Mickey balloons on Main Street and the confetti that falls during the Times Square Ball Drop in New York City have in common?

A. Both concepts were designed by the same person.

B. Both items are made in New York City.

C. Both debuted at the Times Square Ball Drop in New York City.

 AN ESSENTIAL STOP AT A VICTORIAN COFFEE SHOP

Main Street Bakery sits in the center of Main Street and will usually have a line out the door first thing in the morning as overtired parents and rope droppers wait to get their first cup of joe. The bakery serves mostly Starbucks products but also carries some Disney-baked goods and snacks, like Mickey cinnamon rolls and grilled cheese sandwiches with tomato soup. The design and current theme of the bakery convey the aesthetic of a general store with a bakery attached, complete with copper pots and pans hung on the wall behind the counter and the tin ceiling tiles that were popular in Victorian kitchens. There are also some subtle nods to suggest that this bakery contains food and drinks from around the world. Maps of cargo shipments crossing the sea and old photos of people enjoying coffee around the world line the walls.

If you are a member of the Starbucks Rewards program, you can still *earn* rewards and use gift cards at this location; however, you cannot *redeem* rewards or use Starbucks discounts here. After you grab your iced coffee, head outside and take that "Starbies on Main" selfie for your social media post!

HOT DOG HOME RUN!

Casey's Corner is one of the (literal) cornerstones of iconic park food in Magic Kingdom. The quick-service location typically opens around 10:30 a.m. and closes thirty minutes after the park closes in the evening. The late hours mean that it is the perfect spot to grab that last-minute all-beef foot-long hot dog or a Frozen Mint Julep Lemonade for the road. With its proximity to the Hub, this location can get very busy before and after the fireworks show. Save yourself time and the headache of waiting in a long line by using the My Disney Experience app to order your food ahead of time.

My culinary tip for Casey's? Order a side of cheese sauce for your hot dog or fries to upgrade your meal from a hit to a home run! Just remember to give yourself at least thirty minutes to digest before trying to ride Mad Tea Party or Space Mountain.

Extra Magic

★

Casey and baseball go all the way back to a poem written by Ernest L. Thayer in 1888: "Casey at the Bat." While the poem is a nice connection to the timeline of Main Street, "Casey at the Bat" also served as the inspiration for an animated short by the same name that appeared as a segment in Disney's movie *Make Mine Music* in 1946.

BEAT THE HEAT WITH A MINT JULEP

Nothing says refinement like a cold and refreshing mint julep on a hot summer day in Magic Kingdom. Harkening back to the mint julep's popularity in the early 1900s, the nonalcoholic Frozen Mint Julep Lemonade at Casey's Corner is the perfect way to sip on something cool and sweet in between all that water you have been drinking to stay hydrated in the Florida heat.

When you have finished your drink, pat your lips politely with a napkin and remember that Queen Clarisse Renaldi of *The Princess Diaries* would have you hasten, never rush, to your next attraction.

THE MOST DYNAMIC DUO

Standing in the middle of the Hub, looking out toward Main Street with Cinderella Castle behind it, is a statue of Walt Disney and Mickey Mouse. This bronze likeness was created in 1993 by famed Disney legend, animator, and sculptor Blaine Gibson. The statue is called *Partners* and was installed in Magic Kingdom in 1995.

Gibson was the perfect choice to work on this piece since he had worked with Walt Disney personally for years. When asked about the inspiration for the pose of Walt and Mickey, Gibson said, "I chose to depict Walt as he was in 1954. I think that was when Walt was in his prime. It was tough, trying to match the media image of Walt Disney, the one the public knows, to the real Walt, the one we knew. I think Walt is admiring the park, and saying to Mickey, 'Look what we've accomplished together,' because truly they were very much a team through it all. 'Look at all the happy people who have come to visit us today.'"

🍴 DINING WITH THE LOVABLE POOH BEAR

The Crystal Palace is a restaurant most lovingly known for its buffet and character interactions with Winnie the Pooh and friends. Pooh Bear has been a popular character since his first Disney feature film appearance in 1977. His popularity skyrocketed in the 1980s and 1990s, when there were multiple Pooh-related animated series on the Disney Channel, which led to a demand from guests for more merchandise and a place to meet Pooh Bear regularly. The Crystal Palace became that location in 1996 and went on to become one of Disney's longest-running character dining experiences.

Before the theme change for Pooh Bear, The Crystal Palace was a "buffeteria" when the location opened its doors in 1971. "Buffeteria" is a term coined by Disney used to describe a quick-service location that has a line and a layout similar to that of a cafeteria but features more substantial meals and a variety of options like a buffet. The architecture of The Crystal Palace was inspired by many famous greenhouses and Victorian glass buildings of the late 1800s, such as the Palm House at Kew Gardens in England, the New York Crystal Palace, and San Francisco's Conservatory of Flowers in Golden Gate Park. However, if you look closely at the outside of the restaurant, you'll notice the building's design is almost split in two. Facing the front door, you'll see that the left side is grand with its intricate porch columns and gingerbread details, while the right side is more simple, with green-and-white-striped canopies. This split design creates a subtle transition into the French and British colonial architecture that can be found in Adventureland.

CHAPTER 3

Adventureland

As you walk farther away from the hometown comfort of Main Street, the sounds of ragtime music fade and are replaced with the booming of drums as you are transported to the exotic and wild world of Adventureland. Gone are the neat rose bushes lining the walkways of Victorian gardens. Instead, rope bridges carry you to the lush jungle and faraway lands! Adventureland isn't themed after one specific region in the world but finds inspiration in the jungles of the Amazon, the islands of Polynesia and the Caribbean, and distant deserts. Here you can choose your own adventure! Will you float down Rivers of Adventure with a captain who's full of jokes? Soar away on a magic carpet? The choices are endless!

Besides having one of the best views in Magic Kingdom from the top of Swiss Family Treehouse, Adventureland is also full of some of the best tastes in Disney. Dole Whip can be found at two locations, with the traditional flavors at Aloha Isle and some new twists on the classic treat at Sunshine Tree Terrace. On top of that, the storytelling in Adventureland is some of the best in the park. Everywhere—including the park design, restaurants, and queue—is filled with hidden references to all kinds of Disney characters, secret societies, singing birds, and a whole lot of Disney history! Adventureland starts with spring rolls and Dole Whip and ends with pirates and hidden treasure. Now *that's* an adventure! Let's start exploring.

 A SPRING ROLL SPECIALTY!

As you approach the Adventureland bridge, you may notice a surprisingly long line of people waiting at a little cart selling spring rolls. If the aromas haven't enticed you to join the line yet, let me fill you in on a little secret: These are no ordinary spring rolls! One of Magic Kingdom's viral social media food trends, this cart dishes up specialty spring rolls that can change with the season or with special events. Two of the mainstays at the cart are the Cheeseburger Roll and the Pepperoni Pizza Roll. The Cheeseburger Roll contains ground beef and melted cheese and adds some flavors like mustard and pickle to really produce a convincing cheeseburger flavor. It is served with a Thousand Island–type dipping sauce. The Pepperoni Pizza Roll has melted mozzarella cheese and plenty of pepperoni and is paired with a marinara dipping sauce. Each order comes with two rolls and is served piping hot. This isn't really an either-or choice, people. Get both!

THE WORLD'S COOLEST TREEHOUSE

Swiss Family Treehouse is one of a handful of remaining attractions from Magic Kingdom's opening day on October 1, 1971. The "tree" is actually made up of concrete, stucco, and steel, and is carefully designed to look as real and lifelike as possible. This helps the attraction blend in with the foliage of the neighboring Jungle Cruise attraction so you can't see the tree from Main Street. (The treehouse used to be more obvious when Magic Kingdom first opened, but now that surrounding trees have matured, it blends in more.) This massive structure was designed to withstand hurricane-force winds and heavy rain—despite being over 60 feet tall and 90 feet wide! This attraction takes inspiration from the 1960 Disney film *Swiss Family Robinson*. In the movie, the Robinson family becomes stranded on a deserted island and uses salvaged pieces from a shipwreck to create their home. As you travel up and around the treehouse, you'll see the different rooms belonging to the family and how they used parts of the ship and jungle to create their home.

Extra Magic

★

Feeling a sudden urge to yodel? It's not just the fresh air up in Swiss Family Treehouse. The attraction features the song "Swisskapolka" playing from the treehouse organ when you pass the main family room. The song is played multiple times in the original movie and also appears as a special Easter egg audio in the "Yodelberg" episode of *Mickey Mouse* (Season 1, Episode 2).

❓ WHAT IS A *DISNEYODENDRON EXIMUS*?

Morgan "Bill" Evans was an American horticulturist that worked with Disney to create a lot of the landscaping around Disney World. Bill landscaped Disney World's Jungle Cruise attraction and the park's character and animal topiaries. Bill was so taken with the giant fake tree for Swiss Family Treehouse that he even came up with a scientific name for it: *Disneyodendron eximus*.

True or False: "Fake Disney tree" is the correct translation for the Latin name *Disneyodendron eximus*.

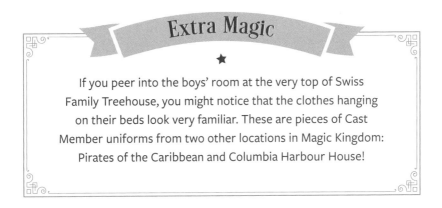

Extra Magic

★

If you peer into the boys' room at the very top of Swiss Family Treehouse, you might notice that the clothes hanging on their beds look very familiar. These are pieces of Cast Member uniforms from two other locations in Magic Kingdom: Pirates of the Caribbean and Columbia Harbour House!

❓ ALL THE WAY TO THE TOP!

As you journey to the top of Swiss Family Treehouse, you can see breathtaking views of every angle of Magic Kingdom—from Cinderella Castle to Big Thunder Mountain Railroad. If you or a member of your party is afraid of heights, it might be best to opt out of ascending the treehouse to see the view . . . however, for those who make it to the top, the view is well worth the climb! While you may have been distracted by the different rooms in the treehouse during your trip to the top, you have actually been climbing a tall set of stairs.

Can you guess how many stairs there are on the way to the top of the treehouse?

    A. 52
    B. 98
    C. 116
    D. 134

SWEET TREATS IN THE SUNSHINE TREE

Now it's time for a nice cold treat! You might have noticed there is frequently a long line of people near the entrance to Adventureland, on the right side, especially during the day. These guests are waiting in line for Sunshine Tree Terrace—one of the homes for Dole Whip! This location is one of two places you can get Dole Whip in Magic Kingdom (with the other location being Aloha Isle—also in Adventureland). Here you can find unique twists on classic Dole Whip with flavors like orange and strawberry and other soft serve flavors like chocolate and vanilla.

Sunshine Tree Terrace also has a large array of sodas to make the perfect float! Yes, you can get a classic root beer float, but since you're in Adventureland, why not be adventurous and try a Fanta Orange Float? Or a crowd favorite, the I Lava You Float—a seasonal float that became so popular it is usually available all year round. This float is made using Fanta Strawberry Soda, passion-fruit-flavored soft serve, and orange Dole Whip and topped with popping candies. That truly sounds like an adventure for the taste buds!

 HOME OF ORANGE BIRD

What's a little bird that looks like an orange doing plastered all around Adventureland? That would be Orange Bird, a character that was made exclusively for Magic Kingdom and also happens to be the favorite character of yours truly. In the late 1960s, the Disney company was looking for companies to sponsor attractions or restaurants in Magic Kingdom. One of the groups that Disney approached to potentially sponsor an attraction in Adventureland was the Florida Citrus Commission. The commission agreed to sponsor the Sunshine Pavilion (what is now known as Walt Disney's Enchanted Tiki Room and Aloha Isle). In exchange, they wanted to use one of Disney's characters as a representative for their orange juice. But Disney was unwilling to sign away licensing rights to an existing character, so they proposed a compromise. Instead of using an existing character, Disney created Orange Bird—a small, orange-colored bird that lives in the Sunshine Tree in Adventureland.

One interesting note about Orange Bird is that he does not speak or sing like other birds found around Disney. Instead, Orange Bird communicates using orange- and yellow-colored thought bubbles. He loves to make new friends and share the importance of fresh fruit in a balanced diet. Adorable!

What is it with birds and citrus groups? Orange Bird was created specifically for use by the Florida Citrus Commission, but did you know that Donald Duck was used as a citrus representative too? The deal came about in 1941, long before Magic Kingdom existed. During supply constraints during World War II, Disney was searching for other ways to monetize its products. Since food products were viewed as wartime essentials, Disney licensed some of its characters to food companies to keep the revenue stream flowing. This included licensing Donald Duck to what was then called Florida Citrus Canners Cooperative. After Walt's death, the company was reviewing contract agreements and assumed that Florida Citrus Canners Cooperative's license for Donald Duck had expired. The citrus cooperative was able to provide a weathered document with proof that Walt and Roy Disney had given them rights with no termination date. The only requirement was that the citrus company would maintain the quality of their product. This contract has silently come to an end in recent years as a result of the changes in branding and marketing for the citrus cooperative.

A TROPICAL SERENADE OF FLAVOR!

In the center of Adventureland near the exit of Enchanted Tiki Room stands Aloha Isle, an outdoor counter service whipping up some classic Dole Whip! Compared to Sunshine Tree Terrace just around the corner, this location has the classic Dole Whip flavors like pineapple, vanilla, and mango. The most popular combinations (and the most Instagrammed) are the classic Pineapple Float and Pineapple Dole Whip Cup. If you want to try something with a little more tropical flare, try a Tropical Serenade. The name is inspired by the original name of the Enchanted Tiki Room show and is made using pineapple-orange-guava juice, coconut soft-serve, and a pineapple upside-down cake pop. Aloha Isle is such a popular location that it opens every day at 10:00 a.m. and remains open until the park closes. Many guests prefer to get their sweet treats from this location in the middle of the day—however, you might want to consider heading over for a treat later in the evening, after the sun has set. The Florida sun can be brutal and make your treat melt too fast. By waiting until the evening hours, it lasts just a bit longer and is a cool way to relax after a long day in the park.

❓ DOLE WHIP'S DEBUT

Believe it or not, there was a time when thousands of Disney fans had to spend their days in the park with no refreshing Dole Whip to enjoy! So how did this frozen concoction come to be? Disney was looking for a new, nondairy treat that could be transported as a dry mix and withstand the blistering Florida heat. The task of creating this product fell to Kathy Westphal, a new UC Davis graduate working at the Dole Technical Center in California. The product was tested and scientifically labeled delicious! Now this frozen treat originally designed for the Disney parks can be found in select grocery stores across America.

What year did Dole Whip debut in Magic Kingdom?

- **A.** 1971
- **B.** 1984
- **C.** 1986
- **D.** 2010

FLOAT TOWARD ~~YOUR DOOM~~ FUN ABOARD JUNGLE CRUISE!

Hop aboard the world-famous Jungle Cruise! This iconic attraction has gone through some major updates since it premiered at the park's opening day in 1971. But the humor and sense of adventure live on! You board a boat captained by a skipper from the Jungle Navigation Company who definitely knows (or definitely does *not* know) their way around the jungle.

Did you know there is more to the ride's backstory than witty skippers? The story starts in 1928, when the founder of the Jungle Navigation Company, Dr. Albert Falls, goes missing. Ten years later, his granddaughter, Alberta Falls, has inherited the company. To make ends meet during the Great Depression, she has converted the cargo company into a tourist trap known as Jungle Cruise.

The wait for this attraction can be pretty long, so try getting on either first thing in the morning or later in the evening. Where else in the world can you see "the backside of water" so enthusiastically displayed?

Park Pointer

★

During the holidays, Jungle Cruise becomes Jingle Cruise!
With holiday music in the queue, holiday-themed jokes
from your jolly skipper, and Christmas decor from a cargo
plane that crashed in the jungle, this is a can't-miss holiday
favorite! Just bear in mind, the attraction may be closed
during the last weeks of October and the middle of January
as the attraction switches its overlay for the season.

? JUNGLE CRUISE SKIPPER WANNABE

Many try to become Jungle Cruise Skippers and many fail. One famous Disney actor applied to become a Jungle Cruise Skipper but was rejected for the role! Can you guess which actor? I'll give you a few hints. This actor was born in Hollywood, Florida, with dreams of performing. After being rejected as a Jungle Cruise Skipper at the age of eighteen, he went on to pursue his degree at the Carnegie Mellon School of Drama before making his way to Broadway. He eventually starred in many Disney films and earned the title of Disney Legend. In fact, he made a callback to the Jungle Cruise rejection during his Disney Legends speech at the D23 Expo in 2022, saying, "To the person that rejected me at Disney casting headquarters . . . please make sure to update my resume to Disney Legend!"

Which famous actor applied to be a Jungle Cruise Skipper and did not get the job?

   A. Josh Gad

   B. Jim Gaffigan

   C. Terry Crews

SKIP OVER TO SKIPPER CANTEEN

Did you know that the best sit-down restaurant in Adventureland is Jungle Navigation Co. LTD Skipper Canteen? That's because it's the only sit-down restaurant in Adventureland! The banter and jokes of the Jungle Cruise attraction have infected the other side of the path—even the menu items at Skipper Canteen aren't safe from a pun or two!

The story goes that the canteen was the home and headquarters of the Falls family, who founded the Jungle Navigation Company. When Alberta eventually took over the family business, she saw an opportunity to repurpose the home as a canteen for the Jungle Navigation Company's Skippers to rest (and work).

If Skippers aren't leading tourists on a tour of the jungle, then they are leading tourists on a tour of flavors from around the world. Skipper Canteen's menu is full of flavor and makes a delicious departure from standard "theme park food." This restaurant has become a fan favorite in Magic Kingdom not just for its decor and theming but also for the incredible food within.

🍴 "TASTES LIKE CHICKEN" BECAUSE IT IS!

Adventure awaits (your taste buds) at Skipper Canteen! This location typically has walk-in seating available in the afternoons if you are looking for a way to beat the jungle heat. Food locations at Magic Kingdom sometimes get a bad rap for being too bland, with choices falling more into the typical park food fare. Skipper Canteen is fighting against that preconceived notion by spicing up its dishes with incredible flavors! Even the menu items get in on the fun with creative names like "Tastes Like Chicken" Because It Is! This dish contains a crispy fried chicken breast with a chili-soy glaze and is served on a bed of jasmine rice with a side of pickled vegetable slaw. Everything else on the menu has a little bit of spice, but hardly any of the items could be considered truly spicy. Skipper Canteen also has some "not-so-secret" menu items, like the Pao de Queijo: Brazilian cheese bread! These delicious bites are gluten-friendly (the bread is made with tapioca flour) and served with a chimichurri cream cheese for dipping. The order is larger than you may think, so this is a delicious appetizer option for sharing. If you think these food items sound amazing, wait till you see what they have for dessert!

🍴 KUNGALOOSH TO YOU!

The delicious options at Skipper Canteen go on for Niles, and Niles, and Niles . . . but you won't want to fill up too much with your appetizers and mains. The dessert is worth saving room for. In particular, you may have noticed a dessert option with a peculiar name: Kungaloosh! This is an African-inspired chocolate cake with caramelized bananas, cashew-caramel ice cream, and a topping of coffee dust. Pronounced phonetically, "Cun-gah-LOOSH" is a word used in the Society of Explorers and Adventurers (which we'll get to later) that serves multiple purposes. It can be similar to "Cheers!" or a toast or can be used as a greeting or goodbye to other society members, similar to how you would use "Aloha" in the Hawaiian language. The word "kungaloosh" appears in multiple places around Disney World. One of the references is hidden on the large map in the Jungle Cruise queue where Alberta Falls makes notes detailing the Adventureland rivers. Here, she uses the word "kungaloosh" as a sign-off.

Extra Magic

★

What is the S.E.A.? The acronym stands for "Society of Explorers and Adventurers"! Disney Imagineers created a fictional group of scientists, explorers, researchers, and artists to further the stories of many attractions and to connect attractions across the parks. The secret S.E.A. was inspired by Pleasure Island's Adventurers Club—a nightclub popular among guests and Imagineers that was open from 1989–2008 in what is now known as Disney Springs. Today, the S.E.A. is focused on the continued exploration of land and sea and is centered around four guiding principles: adventure, romance, discovery, and innovation. Here in Magic Kingdom, Jungle Cruise, Jungle Navigation Co. LTD Skipper Canteen, and Big Thunder Mountain Railroad all contain lore related to this group.

❓ FIND THE FEZ

While inside Jungle Navigation Co. LTD Skipper Canteen, you may notice a few references to the S.E.A. on the artifacts around the wall. According to the lore, Dr. Albert Falls was one of the core members and used Skipper Canteen as a meeting place for the society. In the restaurant, you can still find artifacts belonging to many of the club members. The members of the society would wear a fez during their secret meetings, and these fezzes are displayed in Skipper Canteen outside the society's secret meeting place.

Do you know where to find the fez collection? Choose the correct option:

A. The library
B. The front door
C. The bathrooms

⚙ IT'S A BIRD, IT'S A PLANE, IT'S A FLYING CARPET!

Hold on to your fez, we are outta here! Sitting in the center of Adventureland is The Magic Carpets of Aladdin. Surprisingly enough, this attraction was not placed in Magic Kingdom until almost nine years after *Aladdin* was released in theaters in 1992! *Aladdin*—along with *Beauty and the Beast, Pocahontas,* and *Mulan*—was a box office record breaker, but Disney wanted to place attractions related to the newer movies in its newest park: Disney-MGM Studios Theme Park (now known as Disney's Hollywood Studios). Disney believed that the popularity of these movies would eventually die down. Boy, was it wrong! Instead, the popularity of these films continued to soar because of the emergence of Walt Disney Home Video and the release of these films to VHS. Guests demanded more from Disney World, especially in Magic Kingdom, which was perceived as having fallen behind the times. Disney answered by introducing The Magic Carpets of Aladdin: a simple family-friendly attraction for all ages and any height. Hold on! We are off to Agrabah!

Extra Magic

★

Careful, they spit! The two gold camels just outside The Magic Carpets of Aladdin attraction are recycled props that were used in Aladdin's Royal Caravan parade, which ran in Disney's Hollywood Studios from December 1992 to August 1995. These camels would spit on guests during the parade, and they continue to startle guests near Magic Carpets to this day!

❓ PRINCE OR POSER?

Voice actor Scott Weinger was the original speaking voice of Aladdin and continued playing the character beyond the original movie. He provided the voice of Aladdin for the cartoon series that aired in 1994 on the Disney Channel and in all the direct-to-video movies like *Aladdin: The Return of Jafar* (1994) and *Aladdin and the King of Thieves*

(1996). You might also recognize his voice if you are a video game player. Scott lent his voice to the character of Aladdin in games like *Kingdom Hearts*, *Disney Infinity*, and *CookieRun: Kingdom*. Not too bad for a street rat!

True or False: The original voice actor of Aladdin also is the same voice actor for the safety reminders on The Magic Carpets of Aladdin.

AGRABAH ROYALTY IN ADVENTURELAND

Adventureland is also the place to meet Agrabah royalty! Just across the street from The Magic Carpets of Aladdin is an area called Agrabah Bazaar. The area opened in December 2000 and was designed to be an outdoor gift shop or marketplace just like the marketplace where we first meet Aladdin! It tied in nicely to The Magic Carpets of Aladdin attraction and sold *Aladdin*-themed toys and Jungle Cruise merchandise. Eventually, plans changed for the area, and Agrabah Bazaar became the meet-and-greet location for Aladdin and Jasmine (and a good spot to enjoy a Dole Whip in the shade!). The royal couple is not there all the time, however, as they are busy with the many demands of their kingdom. The couple can usually be found in the bazaar between 10:30 a.m. and 2:00 p.m., but always double-check the My Disney Experience app to verify.

 MEET CLYDE AND CLAUDE!

Let's get to know some very special birds at Magic Kingdom! While there are three Enchanted Tiki Room–themed attractions worldwide, only the one in Magic Kingdom has a very special preshow where two very amusing animatronic toucans welcome you to the magical Sunshine Pavilion. These birds are Clyde and Claude, voiced by actors Dallas McKennon and Sebastian Cabot.

Both actors were no strangers to voice work for the Disney company. McKennon's voice and sound effects can be heard in multiple films like *Lady and the Tramp* (1955), *Mary Poppins* (1964), *Bedknobs and Broomsticks* (1971), and *Sleeping Beauty* (1959), just to name a few. However, most parkgoers will recognize his voice from Big Thunder Mountain Railroad as the prospector who tells you it's best to "hang onto them hats an' glasses, cuz this here's the wildest ride in the wilderness!"

Sebastian Cabot also had experience with Disney projects and can be heard as the narrator for *The Many Adventures of Winnie the Pooh* (1977) and as Bagheera the panther from *The Jungle Book* (1967).

❓ IT'S TIKI TIME!

In the preshow of Enchanted Tiki Room, we see a couple of different tiki gods from Polynesian mythology scattered around the waterfall. When the preshow starts, the waterfall parts and we see the toucans Clyde and Claude sitting on the top of a much larger tiki god called Citrikua. Citrikua is a reference to the original sponsor of the area: the Florida Citrus Commission.

What is Citrikua the god of in Polynesian mythology?

A. Rain

B. Fire

C. Pineapples

D. None of the above

 AN INCREDIBLE ISLAND SHOW

If you've never taken the time to stop by Walt Disney's Enchanted Tiki Room, you cannot call yourself a Disney expert. Even if one of your family members complains and says, "It's just a boring bird show!" take them by the hand and drag them in anyway! (If necessary, use the excuse that it's air-conditioned and a way to take a break from the heat.)

This beautiful show is set in a theater-in-the-round with a run time of just over twelve minutes (not including the preshow). The birds, of course, are the stars, but the rest of Tiki Room is also enchanted, and the entire room comes to life with over 225 animatronic objects!

The most famous song in the show is "The Tiki, Tiki, Tiki Room," and it will probably get stuck in your head for the rest of the day because it was written by Richard and Robert Sherman. The Sherman brothers were the same music masters who wrote the tunes for movies like *Mary Poppins* (1964) and other attractions like "it's a small world." Enchanted Tiki Room is a Disney classic that still has die-hard fans to this day.

? A TIKI TEST

How much do you know about Walt Disney's Enchanted Tiki Room? John Hench was in charge of the original sketches for Enchanted Tiki Room, which opened in 1963 in Disneyland, becoming the very first attraction to feature Audio-Animatronics. John's sketches depicted tropical birds in cages above the seated guests. Upon seeing the concept, Walt assumed John wanted the birds to be real. Walt voiced that they couldn't put birds above the guests because they would poop on them! John reassured Walt that the birds were going to be fake—they'd just *look* real.

At Disney World, Enchanted Tiki Room wasn't always supposed to be what it is today. After some deliberation, the designers scrapped the original idea for the location because they feared people would love the birds and show so much they wouldn't leave!

Do you know what Walt wanted Enchanted Tiki Room to be originally?

A. A Polynesian dance show

B. A water ride through the islands of Hawaii

C. A Polynesian restaurant

D. A thunderstorm-themed rollercoaster

FIND TREASURE IN ADVENTURELAND

Did you know you can join Captain Jack Sparrow's crew for the day and search for treasure around Adventureland? It's called A Pirate's Adventure: Treasure of the Seven Seas. In a small building to your left as you exit the Pirates of the Caribbean ride, you will find The Crow's Nest—the pirate headquarters where you and your crew can choose a pirate map with clues and a magic talisman to find different treasures hidden around Adventureland. There are five missions and maps in total, and it should take you about twenty minutes to complete each mission. If you complete all five missions, you can return to The Crow's Nest to receive a final card signed by the infamous Captain Jack himself! This is a fun and free experience that is available from noon to 6:00 p.m. every day, and you don't have to complete all the challenges in one day, as they have no time limit. So, on a particularly crowded day, if you or your party doesn't feel like standing in line, this is a great option to break up the day. Keep to the code!

MAKE A SWASHBUCKLING SPLASH!

Yo ho, a pirate's life for me! Pirates of the Caribbean in Magic Kingdom opened in 1973—two years after the rest of Adventureland—once Imagineers decided that the popular Disneyland attraction needed a similar version in Disney World.

This ride has one of the most immersive queues in the park! Caribbean Plaza, which surrounds the attraction, is inspired by the Spanish Colonial–style architecture found on the islands of the Greater Antilles, a subregion of the Caribbean. As you step into the Pirates of the

Caribbean attraction queue, you pass through what seems to be a large citadel fortress dating back to the 1600s. The fortress was designed to be reminiscent of the Castillo San Felipe del Morro in San Juan, Puerto Rico. As you venture through the queue, you pass through an armory full of gunpowder, cannons, and jail cells before eventually heading down the ramps toward the boats at Pirate's Cove. You then board one of these ships and set off into the caves below the fort to escape a pirate attack. The ride lasts for almost nine minutes and has scenes filled with animatronic pirates and scallywags. In total, there are over 120 Audio-Animatronics throughout the entire ride. Aye, that be impressive!

Park Pointer

★

Attraction wait times ebb and flow like the tide. So, when is the best time to try and ride Pirates of the Caribbean? On a standard park day, the wait times can vary between twenty minutes and fifty minutes with the busiest times being around 11:00 a.m. and 5:00 p.m. The slowest times are in the afternoon around 2:00 p.m. during the midday parade and in the evening after 6:00 p.m.

🍴 A PORT OF CALL FOR HUNGRY PIRATES

Hidden away in the back of Caribbean Plaza just across from the Pirates of the Caribbean attraction is Tortuga Tavern, a quick-service location that operates seasonally and is typically only open for limited hours during peak times. When it is open, it provides a nice additional option for dining in Adventureland. Tortuga Tavern has an inside seating area and a large outside patio and is the perfect spot to relax during busy park days.

The menu has changed multiple times over the years, and it seems that every time it opens for peak season the menu has rotated again! Previous menus included standard park fare like turkey legs, hot dogs, chili cheese fries, and brisket sandwiches. However, during the fiftieth anniversary of Magic Kingdom, the menu featured a teriyaki burger and sweet-and-sour chicken tenders—both hidden gems! As usual, the My Disney Experience app is the best place to see if the location is open and what menu items are available.

? GHOSTLY VOICES

One of the most famous lines in the Pirates of the Caribbean attraction is the eerie, ghostly cry heard echoing among the remains of lost souls in the caves: "Dead men tell no tales!" This spooky voice was performed by voice actor Paul Frees, whose voice is in one of the Pirates of the Caribbean movies! In *Pirates of the Caribbean: At World's End*, at the 32:29 minute mark, the ride's audio makes a brief twenty-second cameo. The faint sound of "Yo ho, a pirate's life for me" can be heard, along with the voice of the original Pirate Captain and some pirate laughter.

Paul Frees's voice is also featured in a different attraction at Magic Kingdom. Can you guess which one?

A. Big Thunder Mountain Railroad

B. Haunted Mansion

C. Walt Disney's Enchanted Tiki Room

Extra Magic

★

A hidden nod to Perry, the famous animated platypus from the Disney Channel show *Phineas and Ferb*, is hidden in an area located just beyond the Adventureland-Frontierland archway to the right of the Pirates of the Caribbean attraction entrance, toward the attraction's bathrooms. It almost looks like a pirate garage sale; however, these are items that belong to Calypso, the sea goddess! You'll see treasures, skulls, and items from around the world. As you stand in front of the display, look to the cabinet on the right bottom shelf, and you'll see a smiling, happy idol with a beard. Look on the platter just below him, and a small platypus skull wearing a fedora is hidden among the treasures. Another item hidden among the curios is an item with the initials of "K.P." in reference to another animated adventurer: Kim Possible!

CHAPTER 4

Frontierland

As you make your way through the subtle transition from Adventureland to Frontierland, you'll notice that the drums have given way to banjos, and lush jungles have been replaced with cacti. The theming of Frontierland draws inspiration from the vistas, rivers, and plains of the American Southwest—the lands west of the Mississippi River. In this land, Southwest lore and stories come to life as attractions, hidden Easter eggs, and larger-than-life characters.

Frontierland pays tribute to the pioneers who shaped the West over the years and is full of the same wild spirit that roams the American Southwest. At Tiana's Bayou Adventure, you have to brave a 52-foot plunge. If that wasn't enough, you face bats, a cave-in, and a careening mine train in Big Thunder Mountain Railroad! If this is a little *too* Wild West for you, Grizzly Hall has a band of friendly bears that will be happy to have you "until the bear end." Food flavors in Frontierland shift to Tex-Mex fare and Southern-inspired cooking. Whether you're in the mood for some nacho and rice bowls or some New Orleans gumbo and beignets, you won't have to worry about traveling on an empty stomach while exploring the Wild West. So, saddle up and begin your ride into the wilderness!

GRUB AT GOLDEN OAK OUTPOST

Howdy, partner! You've stumbled upon Golden Oak Outpost, which is considered the very edge of the frontier (literally and figuratively). For the longest time, this location was a seasonal quick-service window that would open up on busy weekends and during peak season months with very basic fried-food options like chicken nuggets, French fries, and the occasional mini corn dogs. With Princess Tiana being the newest neighbor in town, the Outpost menu has changed to feature Southern comfort food with a little extra flavor. Shrimp, gumbo, hot honey chicken, sweet potato fries, and, of course, Tiana's famous "man-catching" beignets are all featured on this revamped menu. These beignets can't be found anywhere else in the park! While the food is unlikely to pass any test from a true Louisianan, this location does deliciously diversify the flavor palate of Frontierland.

THE GREAT BEIGNET BATTLE

While Golden Oak Outpost is the only place in Disney World to grab some of Tiana's "man-catching" beignets, you can find the delicious treats at several other locations on Disney property. The arrival of the beignets at Golden Oak Outpost is one of the first times that beignets have been sold regularly at Magic Kingdom. For many long years, the only previous option for beignets at Disney World was to make a special trip to Disney's Port Orleans Resort—French Quarter (which is worth the trip if you have the time).

With various delicious hot pockets of dough dusted with sugar flying around, you may be asking, which is the best one? The main difference between the beignets at Magic Kingdom and the ones at French Quarter is that Golden Oak Outpost's come in a square shape, while the beignets at French Quarter come in a Mickey shape. Disney scientists and specialists agree: Any food product in the shape of Mickey Mouse will taste at least 27 percent better than non-Mickey-shaped food (this research has been exclusively conducted by yours truly). However, the real answer to where the best beignets can be found is simple: The best beignets are the ones you are holding in your hands!

MCDONALD'S IN THE WILD WEST?

Without fail, on any given day in Magic Kingdom, you will pass by Golden Oak Outpost only to overhear someone say: "I remember when they used to serve McDonald's fries in that spot." It's true! In the late 1990s and early 2000s, McDonald's and Disney had multiple partnerships. One of those partnerships was the Frontierland Kiosk, which operated from 1997 to 2007. This food kiosk was placed in the same spot where Golden Oak Outpost is today (though it looked nothing like the current building). The original design resembled a red stagecoach with broken yellow wheels. Seeing their predicament, the owners of this coach made the most of the bad situation and opened up shop. Frontierland Kiosk only sold McDonald's fries and soda, but that little cart made such a big impression that guests still remember it to this day.

CELEBRATING BAYOU-STYLE

We are going down the bayou! Tiana has officially moved into Frontierland, bringing a little bit of her New Orleans flair to the frontier. During the opening of Tiana's Bayou Adventure, there was a little confusion on what the storyline of this attraction was. Were you searching for spices? Was it just a boat ride? What is Tiana's Foods? Most of the story is explained in the attraction queue through a series of small details and clues.

This attraction takes place after the events of *The Princess and the Frog* movie. Tiana's restaurant opened, and she is now expanding her food empire with the opening of Tiana's Foods. According to the story, Tiana's Foods is an employee-owned food cooperative located in an old salt mine just outside New Orleans featuring a boutique farm, teaching and test kitchens, and a manufacturing site for Tiana's line of original hot sauces. When you enter into the story, Mardi Gras season has just begun, and Tiana is getting ready to throw the biggest party of the year. There's just one problem: Every band in New Orleans is booked for Mardi Gras! You, along with Tiana and Louis the Alligator, journey into the bayou in search of a band of musical critters to play at the big party. This band includes animals and amphibians of all sizes—and the journey to find them contains drops and surprises! The trip culminates in a huge celebration at the end of the ride to welcome you to the party, along with a special thank-you from Tiana because "your very special spice makes us complete."

HOW FAST IS THAT WATER FALLING?

On Tiana's Bayou Adventure, guests will encounter a few dips on their journey through the bayou before ascending up the lift hill to plummet down a 52-foot water flume toward the end of the attraction.

What is the max speed you reach as you plummet down that last hill in Tiana's Bayou Adventure?

- **A.** 30 mph
- **B.** 60 mph
- **C.** 40 mph

 **MEET THE BAND!**

When designing an attraction, Disney Imagineers love to come up with backstories and personalities for their creation. This holds true for Tiana's Bayou Adventure, where almost every animal has a backstory of some sort. The Imagineers also paid tribute to the different types of music you would hear around New Orleans with each of the three groups of critters playing different types of music.

★ The first group of furry friends that you encounter play zydeco, a genre of music that originated in southwest Louisiana. It's a blend of the blues, R&B, and the music of Louisiana Creoles. The critters in this part of the band are Byhalia the Beaver, Rufus the Turtle, Apollo the Raccoon, Gritty the Rabbit, Timoléon the Otter, and Beau the Possum.

★ The second group of critters that you will encounter play Rara! Rara is a type of festival music that originated in Haiti and is used in street processions. These band members are Octavia the Bobcat, Pawpaw the Bobcat, Phina the Gray Fox, and the Black Bear family of Claude, Bernadette, and Sebastian.

★ The last, but certainly not least, group of critters that you encounter on your journey are actually amphibians. The frogs Felipe, Mayra, Mondo, and Isabel are masters of Afro-Cuban jazz, bringing jazzy sounds with a complex rhythm to the deepest part of the bayou. Listen carefully as you travel through the ride, and you can hear how each of these music genres is distinctly different but combines beautifully (like a big pot of jumbo)!

Extra Magic

★

There is one other critter you should keep an eye on while exploring Tiana's Bayou Adventure! His name is Lari the Armadillo, and out of the nineteen critters in the attraction, he is one of the few that is not a musician. Lari, however, does help the other critters as he is a fixer, finder, and "junk man" of sorts in the bayou. For example, Lari supplied Gritty the Rabbit with a new washboard made out of a license plate. Lari will firmly state that the license plate he gave to Gritty was not being used by anybody; however, the delivery car in the queue just so happens to be missing its license plate. As a bonus, there is a note in the queue from one of Tiana's employees that reads, "Missing license plate! If found, please contact Avery." If Lari acquires something for you, it might be best to not ask too many questions about where it came from!

 DIRECT FROM NEW ORLEANS

Located just outside the queue of Tiana's Bayou Adventure is a little gift shop called Critter Co-op. Inside you will find plushies, shirts, and dolls—but also spice! Have you ever wanted to know how Mama Odie's hot sauce from her bathtub pot of gumbo tastes? Well, now you can find out! You can also find seasonings from Dooky Chase's Restaurant in New Orleans. Chef Leah Chase was the owner of Dooky

Chase's Restaurant, and her story and spirit served as the inspiration for Tiana's character in the movie! While Leah was nicknamed the "Queen of Creole Cuisine," she was also an activist and played a crucial role in the civil rights movement in New Orleans. Critter Co-op has spices direct from Leah Chase's restaurant and is one of the only places that you can purchase them outside of Dooky Chase's Restaurant!

LEGENDS COME TO LIFE AT PECOS BILL'S

On your long travels through the frontier, you might be thinking it's time to "rustle up some grub" and just so happen to stumble upon Pecos Bill Tall Tale Inn and Cafe. Usually by the time guests step into Pecos Bill's, they're so hungry they don't even realize they are surrounded by items belonging to American folklore heroes! Pecos Bill, who is known for being "the toughest critter west of the Alamo" runs this inn and cafe. On the walls inside the restaurant is the in-depth backstory of Pecos Bill and how the restaurant came to be (in true Frontierland fashion, the story is written on dried hide). As the story goes, Pecos Bill's spot was a popular hangout for his legendary friends. It became tradition that when each of his friends would visit, they would leave him a gift. Pecos later hung up these items on the walls with inscriptions to say exactly who they were from.

The food served in Tall Tale Inn and Cafe has changed quite a lot over the years, but for the most part has been inspired by Tex-Mex cuisine. Recently, the menu went through a large change and now serves up items like steamed tamales, create-your-own nacho bowls and rice bowls, double chili con queso burgers, and grilled masa flatbreads. If you are a true fan of Tex-Mex, though, try the Sweet Corn Mousse! The dessert is molded into a corn shape, drizzled with white chocolate, and sprinkled with raspberry powder. This gives it the appearance of elote (Mexican street corn) but has all the sweetness you could want. Tall tales need tall orders!

? TALL TALE ROUNDUP

There are multiple items inside Pecos Bill Tall Tale Inn and Cafe from some of Pecos's friends.

Throughout the restaurant, many items have inscriptions denoting who they belong to. Can you match the folklore item to the hero?

Paul Bunyan	Coonskin Cap
Lone Ranger	Tin Pot Hat
Casey Jones	Engineer Equipment
Buffalo Bill	Axe
Johnny Appleseed	Mask and Silver Bullet
Davy Crockett	Show Boots

IT'S THE WILDEST RIDE IN THE WILDERNESS!

Hold on to them hats and glasses, cause it's gonna be a bumpy ride on Big Thunder Mountain Railroad! Big Thunder is a roller coaster that takes you on an out-of-control train ride through the gold mines in the mining town of Tumbleweed. Opening September 23, 1980, Big Thunder was the second roller coaster built in Magic Kingdom. Known for its tight turns and small dips, this track has a momentum that makes it seem like you are going really fast. In actuality, the coaster only reaches a max speed of 36 miles per hour! This coaster does not have any super intense drops compared to Tiana's Bayou Adventure or TRON Lightcycle / Run, which means that it is a great stepping stone for smaller thrill seekers.

 COURAGE FOR THE RIDE

Five trains ride the track for Big Thunder Mountain Railroad, each with its own name.

Which is not one of the Big Thunder Mountain Railroad train names?

- **A.** U.B. Bold
- **B.** U.B. Strong
- **C.** U.R. Courageous
- **D.** U.R. Daring
- **E.** I.M. Brave
- **F.** I.M. Fearless
- **G.** I.B. Hearty

THE UNTOLD LORE OF THE MINING GHOST TOWN

While Big Thunder Mountain is an exciting roller coaster, many guests pass right by the in-depth theming and storytelling that takes place in the queue and on the ride. Here is the story of Big Thunder: In 1880, the Big Thunder Mining Company, owned by Barnabas T. Bullion, set up a mining town in Big Thunder Mountain (located in Arizona) and called it Tumbleweed. Bullion descended from a mining family. Through his connections, he met other explorers and adventurers, eventually joining the S.E.A. He felt that mining was his birthright and looked for gold throughout the world, even seeking out the legendary city of gold, El Dorado.

When he gained possession of the Big Thunder Mining Company, he tore up the mountain in search of more and more gold. The Native Americans in the neighboring villages warned Bullion that his greed would anger the spirit of Big Thunder. Bullion ignored their warnings, even as supernatural happenings plagued the town of Tumbleweed. Men went missing, mine shafts collapsed, and eventually drought reduced Tumbleweed to a ghost town. After Bullion passed away and mining began to cease, the spirit of Big Thunder returned rain to the town, almost flooding it in the process. So, when you hop aboard the mine train, you'll weave in and out of collapsed mine shafts and the now-flooded town of Tumbleweed!

Park Pointer

★

If you find yourself in Frontierland during the middle of the day, be sure to check the time! The afternoon Magic Kingdom parade starts in Frontierland and makes its way toward Liberty Square and Main Street. The streets of Frontierland are a little less crowded compared to Main Street, so it's a great spot to watch the action. This is also the ideal spot for viewing evening parades, like Mickey's Very Merry Christmas Party or Mickey's Not-So-Scary Halloween Party. The lower light levels in Frontierland really allow the lighting of the floats to come alive! Check the My Disney Experience app for all parade times.

WHICH COASTER IS THE LONGEST?

Magic Kingdom has added a few roller coasters other than Big Thunder Mountain Railroad over the years, totaling five coasters in all.

Which coaster is the longest measured by ride time?

- **A.** TRON Lightcycle / Run
- **B.** Seven Dwarfs Mine Train
- **C.** The Barnstormer
- **D.** Big Thunder Mountain Railroad
- **E.** Space Mountain

HOP ABOARD THE FRONTIERLAND TRAIN!

Sometimes you just need a break from the crowds to rest for a spell. What's more relaxing than a scenic ride around the park? In the center of Frontierland is Frontierland Train Station, where you can hop aboard Walt Disney World Railroad. If you decide to take a ride on the train, head up the stairs to the platform located just above the queue for Tiana's Bayou Adventure. A new train arrives at the station every four-to-seven minutes, and it takes about twenty-to-thirty minutes to complete the full tour. If you end up waiting for the next train, be sure to check out the detailed decor in the station that includes everything from luggage to wilderness supplies to maps.

Once you're on the train and you pull out of Frontierland Station, you will pass the flooded town of Tumbleweed. You might even catch a glimpse of one of those out-of-control trains whizzing by! Along the tracks as you head out of Frontierland, you will pass some "wildlife" like rattlesnakes, roadrunners, and an alligator or two as you approach the Native American village on the outskirts of town.

Park Pointer

★

If you happen to be in Frontierland when a severe weather event occurs, Magic Kingdom Cast Members will sometimes use the Country Bear Musical Jamboree theater as a storm shelter. This is usually in the event of severe lightning, which is a pretty regular occurrence in Central Florida. If this does occur, the show will be suspended until it is safe for guests to move around the park again.

 A "BEARY" GOOD SHOW

"Howdy, folks! Welcome to the one and only original Country Bear Musical Jamboree!" This show, located in Grizzly Hall, was one of the opening day attractions in 1971 (known then as Country Bear Jamboree), but in July 2024, the entire show was given a major facelift including all-new songs, costumes, lighting, decor in the queue—and, of course, fur. While there were many reasons for this much-needed upgrade, one of the main ones related to the song choices. Many of the songs in the original attraction were released in the 1960s and 1970s. While they were popular country music songs then, most of them did not withstand the test of time. After fifty-three years, it was time for a change.

To avoid a similar fate as the songs in the previous show, Imagineering decided to use Disney classics that have had lasting power—such as "The Bare Necessities" from *The Jungle Book* and "Kiss the Girl" from *The Little Mermaid*—with a country twist! The story of the new show starts in the queue where you see display cases showing pictures and memorabilia from the years the bears spent touring the world, along with awards and records from their musical ventures. The new show is themed around the idea that the bear band has returned home to where they first got their start. Country genres like Americana, country pop, bluegrass, and rockabilly are represented in the show. So, clap your paws and sing along; the bears are going to put on a very entertaining show!

Toward the middle of Country Bear Musical Jamboree, the MC, Henry, comes out to introduce the next performance, saying, "Our next performer used to play with the Mineral Kings." This is not a reference to a real band, but a real-life Disney location that the original show was supposed to occupy. In 1965, Walt Disney acquired property in the Sequoia National Forest in California with plans to create a ski lodge that would be called Mineral King Ski Resort. One of the original features of this resort was a show to be performed by singing animatronic bears. When the plans for the ski resort fell through, Disney Imagineering had already developed so much of the show that they decided to keep the concept and move it to their new park in Florida. There's a bit more to the Mineral Kings, but you'll have to wait until the Tomorrowland chapter to find out!

 ## COUNTRY SONGS AND DISNEY LEGENDS

The new Country Bear Musical Jamboree has some subtle nods to Disney Legends like Dick Van Dyke and Wally Boag. Around the middle of the show, a brown bear named Ernest "the Dude" appears with a fiddle sitting on his knee wearing a straw hat, blue bow tie, and yellow-, red-, and orange-striped vest to fiddle the fastest version of "Supercalifragilisticexpialidocious" this side of the Mississippi, honoring Dick Van Dyke's character Bert from the movie *Mary Poppins*. The mother-of-pearl on the fiddle is also a reference to the Pearly

Band that performs with Mary and Bert in the movie during the song "Supercalifragilisticexpialidocious."

The show's second reference appears when Terrence, aka Shaker, comes out on stage to perform the song "Fixer Upper" from the movie *Frozen* (2013). Terrence's costume, with its large cowboy hat and fuzzy chaps, pays homage to Disney Legend Wally Boag. Wally was the longest-running character performer in the Golden Horseshoe Revue, performing over 40,000 shows during his career in Disneyland. He is also credited with helping to bring the show from Disneyland to Walt Disney World in 1971, opening as the Diamond Horseshoe Revue. In the show, Wally primarily played the part of Pecos Bill, and Terrence's costume is fashioned after Wally's Pecos Bill costume. Wally became world-famous in this outfit and even made an appearance on *The Muppet Show*.

Park Pointer

★

Frontierland is a great place to watch the fireworks in Magic Kingdom. While you won't get to experience the projections on Cinderella Castle and Main Street, you still get an amazing view of the fireworks themselves, with speakers blasting the show music and hardly any crowd of people around you. A couple of the best vantage points for watching the show are near the water's edge looking in the direction of Haunted Mansion or from the bridge leading from Pecos Bill Tall Tale Inn and Cafe to Big Thunder Mountain Railroad. Or, if you head toward Liberty Square to where the boardwalk starts near the river, there is a speaker on the corner that pipes the show music into the area, and there's a great view of the fireworks and of Haunted Mansion too.

When Walt Disney was diagnosed with a tumor on his lung, he underwent an attempt to surgically remove it on November 6, 1966. After his surgery, and despite his diagnosis, Walt Disney would still go to the office and the Disney Studios to check in on current projects. During what would be one of his last visits, he stopped in to check on Marc Davis—one of Walt Disney's Nine Old Men (a group of core Disney animators)—and the "Bear Project." As Marc told the story, Marc showed him the newest illustrations and progress with the bear band, cracking jokes and making Walt Disney laugh. Marc reminisces that they laughed and cut up like the good ol' days. Walt Disney might have laughed a little too hard, as he was reported to say he wasn't feeling well and called a company car to take him home. As he left Marc Davis's office, he turned and said, "Goodbye, Marc." In that moment, Marc Davis knew that he would not see Walt again, as Walt was known for never saying goodbye. Walt Disney passed away a few days later.

HIDDEN HISTORY IN THE QUEUE

Country Bear Musical Jamboree also lived in Disneyland once upon a time—when it was known as Country Bear Jamboree. This attraction closed in Disneyland in 2001 to make way for The Many Adventures of Winnie the Pooh. Adjacent to the original location in Disneyland is a quick-service location called Hungry Bear Restaurant. When you enter into the lobby of the attraction, immediately to your right is a small display case and in it a napkin from Hungry Bear Restaurant containing notes and scribbles of a set list for the show you are about to see. Over in Disneyland, the soundtrack of this show now plays at Hungry Bear Restaurant, where the bear band brainstormed their set list.

Another thing to look for in the queue area are small illustrations of multiple bears that do not appear in the show. These illustrations are concept art sketches, created by Marc Davis for the original show. Copies of these illustrations were brought out of the Disney archives and added to the queue during the 2024 remodel. These illustrations honor the original show and even some of the elements of a show that never was.

Park Pointer

★

Since 2020, the ever-helpful Guest Experience Team, an extension of Disney's Guest Relations, can be seen wearing dark blue and stationed under dark blue umbrellas throughout the park. These Cast Members are great points of reference and assistance with helping you navigate the My Disney Experience app. If you find yourself in need of Guest Relations, go to one of these locations first before walking all the way back to Main Street. You might still need to make the trip if the tools needed to assist you are not available via the mobile technology accessible to the team under the umbrella. The Guest Experience location in Frontierland is typically located on the walkway across from Frontier Trading Post.

 WESTWARD HO (FOR BREAKFAST)!

Located across the walkway from Pecos Bill's toward the bridge that leads you to Big Thunder Mountain Railroad is an outside vending location that serves snacks. The cart is called Westward Ho and is one of the few locations to open up at 9:30 a.m. with a small selection of breakfast items. This is a rare find because there are very few locations that offer a quick-serve breakfast! You can get biscuit sandwiches with fried chicken, half-egg omelets, or cinnamon-sugar donut holes—all of which pair nicely with Joffrey's Coffee Cold Brew!

After 11:00 a.m., Westward Ho serves mini corn dogs, candied bacon skewers, and jalapeño poppers stuffed with nacho cheese and served with ranch dressing. The outside portion of this kiosk is where you can find other standard park fare like popcorn, water, and other bottled beverages.

FRONTIER TRADING POST

Searching for the newest mystery trading pins or looking to find the largest selection of Disney trading pins in Magic Kingdom? Frontier Trading Post is the place for all your pin-trading needs. This quaint little shop is decorated to look like a general store from the early American frontier. Cast Members are happy to chat with you about the newest pin. If you have a little pin collector in your party, this may be a spot you want to pop into to find their next favorite souvenir.

★

Pin trading has become a huge part of Disney culture with many guests participating in this fun tradition of swapping pins and adding to their personal collection. Pin trading began in October 1999 in Disney World before spreading to other Disney parks around the world by 2000. it was only meant to last for the millennium celebration at Disney parks worldwide, but due to the overwhelming response, pin trading grew into a tradition at Disney properties that continues to this day!

CHAPTER 5

Liberty Square

Welcome to Liberty Square! This land is a celebration of the founding of America and of the American spirit. While Liberty Square is one of the smallest lands in the park, it contains some of the best Easter eggs and is full of nods to the history of both Disney and America.

The origins of Liberty Square can be found in Walt Disney's love for history. Around 1956, Walt imagined a new area for Disneyland that would pay tribute to American history and feature an attraction that focused on the American presidents. Due to constraints in Disneyland (both spatial and technological), the idea was shelved—but not forgotten! Instead, when the time came to work on the plans for Magic Kingdom, Walt made sure that a more permanent home for the American historical land he imagined was included.

Unfortunately, Walt would not live to see the fulfillment of his dream in Disney World. Liberty Square opened with the rest of Magic Kingdom in 1971, ready to join in the commemoration of the United States bicentennial five years later. Liberty Square is an immersion into honoring the past, present, and future of the United States!

 PAYING HOMAGE TO US PRESIDENTS

The Hall of Presidents was conceived as an attraction that would be presented at Disneyland and the 1964 New York World's Fair. Originally titled One Nation Under God, the attraction was unable to secure any sponsorship or funding and was shelved before it came to fruition. Walt's vision for the attraction had once again progressed far beyond the available technology of the time. Instead of a grand Hall of Presidents, Walt worked with Disney Imagineering to create an Audio-Animatronic of one president: Abraham Lincoln. This accomplishment turned into the popular Great Moments with Mr. Lincoln attraction at Disneyland. Thanks to this success, the idea of The Hall of Presidents was revisited for the creation of Magic Kingdom and became an opening day attraction. It continues to be updated to include every American president elected to office.

The attraction is an indoor air-conditioned theater that holds seven hundred people. The immersive experience of the show and the history begins in the lobby queue area. There are multiple displays featuring items on loan from Walt Disney Archives, the Library of Congress, and private collections from the families of presidents. These items change depending on availability, so make sure you check out the displays each time.

The show itself is broken up into three distinct parts:

1. Part one presents a brief history of the founding of the United States along with the creation of the office of the president.
2. The second part of the show highlights the way the office of the president shaped America, focusing especially on President Lincoln (for you Disneyland nerds, this part includes a portion of the original Great Moments with Mr. Lincoln attraction!).
3. Finally, the show emphasizes the importance of American people choosing their leadership and celebrates the liberties provided by the United States Constitution before culminating in the dramatic entrance of every American president. Each president is shown in animatronic form across the stage in various poses, acknowledging their introduction as they are listed in order of election. President George Washington gives a few words before we hear the current president recite the oath of office and share some brief remarks.

While many view this show as simply a place to escape the Florida heat or a passing rain shower, it is truly uplifting and inspiring. In fact, it's hard to leave without a greater appreciation for the office of the president.

NAME THAT PRESIDENT!

One of the most unique aspects about The Hall of Presidents attraction is that the current president of the United States recites the oath of office and gives some brief remarks near the end of the show. Nowadays, these remarks are recorded by the presidents themselves specifically for Disney—but that wasn't always the case.

Which president was the first to record their speaking part for The Hall of Presidents?

A. George Washington

B. Abraham Lincoln

C. Joe Biden

D. Bill Clinton

Extra Magic

★

The invite list for the 1971 opening ceremonies at Magic Kingdom included United States President Richard Nixon. Due to security concerns, President Nixon was not able to be present. In his absence, he sent Roy Disney the American flag that flew above the White House on October 1, 1971, to be used during the dedication day on October 25, 1971. A quote from Nixon's letter states, "As it is raised in Town Square may it represent our faith in the American dream which is so much in evidence at Walt Disney World." This same flag and note from President Nixon were on display for the fiftieth anniversary of The Hall of Presidents, in the entrance queue area.

🍴 SOMETHING TO BE THANKFUL FOR EVERY DAY OF THE YEAR

Since we are in Liberty Square, we have to celebrate that all-important American holiday: Thanksgiving! Thanksgiving was a part of early American colonial history and was formally recognized in 1789 with a proclamation from President George Washington. It didn't become an official legal holiday until 1870, when it was signed into law by President Ulysses Grant.

Extra Magic

★

While there are nods to famous figures from American history hidden throughout Liberty Tree Tavern's six dining rooms, there is also a reference to a particular animated mouse. In the Benjamin Franklin dining room, a bookshelf sits to the right of the staircase. On the very top of that bookshelf, peeking around the books, is a mouse. This mouse is not Mickey—it is Amos, the mouse from the animated short *Ben and Me*. In the short, Amos helps give Benjamin Franklin the ideas for bifocal lenses, the Franklin stove, and many other projects. Looking to watch this short for yourself? *Ben and Me* can be watched on Disney+ as part of the show *The Liberty Story*, which also includes some segments by Walt Disney and a clip of the movie *Johnny Tremain* (1957).

No one celebrates this grand American holiday better than Liberty Tree Tavern, where a Thanksgiving dinner with all the fixings is served family-style 365 days of the year. What a great thing to be thankful for! This restaurant has changed very little in the time that it has been in Magic Kingdom. The wood paneling, large fireplaces, and candelabra chandeliers give the feeling of a tavern from 1776. Each of the six dining rooms is decorated to represent a famous person from American history: George Washington, Betsy Ross, Thomas Jefferson, Paul Revere, Benjamin Franklin, and John Paul Jones. Your host or hostess will tell you the significance of the room you are sitting in and which figure it takes inspiration from. Be sure to look at the decor and artifacts, as they are representative of one of these key figures in American history.

The meal is three courses, served in an all-you-care-to-enjoy style. The first course is Declaration Salad, a house salad with mixed greens, cranberries, apples, cheese, and a house-made dressing, along with delectable buttery rolls! The main course is the Patriot's Platter, serving up well-seasoned pot roast, roast turkey, oven-roasted pork, mashed potatoes, green beans, herbed stuffing, and house-made macaroni and cheese. If you find yourself wanting another helping of anything in particular, just let your server know and they will bring more. One word of advice: Try your hardest to leave room for dessert (Ooey Gooey Toffee Cake)! While this meal is delicious and well worth the price, afterward you might catch yourself dozing off just like you might after your actual Thanksgiving dinner. Plan accordingly and order coffee with dessert!

EVEN THE TREES ARE CAST MEMBERS!

Just like every Cast Member at Disney has a role to play, so too does the foliage! The giant southern live oak Liberty Tree sits at the center of Liberty Square. The tree is estimated to be more than 140 years old and was transported from the edge of Walt Disney World property to the center of Liberty Square during the construction of Magic Kingdom. The tree is a representation of a real tree located in Boston, Massachusetts, that was a gathering place for patriots who called themselves the Sons of Liberty during the years leading up to and during the Revolutionary War.

The tree was famously depicted in the Disney movie *Johnny Tremain*, which is based on the Esther Forbes historical novel published in 1943. In the movie, multiple lanterns are hung on the boughs of the tree following the Boston Tea Party. Thirteen lanterns also hang from the branches of the tree in Liberty Square, representing the original thirteen colonies.

 **LET FREEDOM RING**

The Liberty Bell in Philadelphia rang on September 17, 1787, to announce the ratification of the United States Constitution. Two hundred years later, the Disney company decided it was fitting for Magic Kingdom to have its very own Liberty Bell in the center of Liberty Square in honor of the bicentennial celebration of America. Disney reached out to Foy Bryant, who owned a replica of the Liberty Bell and used it for parades and school education sessions across California. Foy and the Disney company came to an agreement, and his bell was loaned to the park.

On September 17, 1987, a small parade and bell-ringing ceremony took place. The bell-ringing ceremony was led by a Cast Member dressed as Benjamin Franklin, with Mickey and Minnie Mouse ringing the bell promptly at 4:00 p.m., the same time as the signing of the Constitution and in tandem with other bells across the United States in celebration of the bicentennial. Afterward, the bell became a popular icon within the park, leading the Disney company to commission their own Liberty Bell using the same mold as the original Liberty Bell. It was installed in its current location in 1989 just before Independence Day.

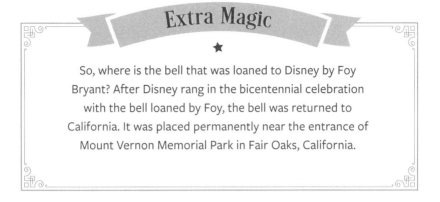

Extra Magic

★

So, where is the bell that was loaned to Disney by Foy Bryant? After Disney rang in the bicentennial celebration with the bell loaned by Foy, the bell was returned to California. It was placed permanently near the entrance of Mount Vernon Memorial Park in Fair Oaks, California.

? TWO VERY POPULAR BELLS

The Liberty Bell in Magic Kingdom has enjoyed quite a reception . . . so much so that more people visit the Liberty Bell in Magic Kingdom than visit the original Liberty Bell in Philadelphia. Or do they?

True or False: The bell in Walt Disney World is visited more than the original Liberty Bell in Philadelphia.

 TWO IF BY SEA

Liberty Square contains many nods to American historical events, such as the legendary ride of Paul Revere. In case you fell asleep in your history class, here is a quick refresher. On April 18, 1775, Paul Revere, a member of the Sons of Liberty, undertook a horseback ride through the Massachusetts Bay Colony, warning other patriots of the British Army's arrival. Lanterns were also hung in the Old North Church steeple to signal the direction that the army was coming from: "one if by land, two if by sea." On that night, two lanterns were placed in the steeple, and Paul Revere made his famous ride. In Liberty Square, a reference to that moment in American history is hidden in one of the windows!

To find the lanterns, head to the seating area behind Liberty Square Market, near the stroller parking area for Haunted Mansion. Look toward the red brick wall, where you'll see a rounded turret with a circular window on the first floor. Located just above that circular window is a rectangular window with two lanterns. Now all you need is a horse!

🍴 LET'S TALK TURKEY

Liberty Square Market is an outdoor seating area with a covered market stall located next to The Hall of Presidents. Here you can find the most debated Disney snack of all time: the turkey leg! The concept of the turkey leg snack was made popular in the 1970s, as Renaissance fairs started to appear across America. Disney was looking for new snacks and food options in its park and decided to give the fair food a try—this on-the-go snack was introduced in Magic Kingdom in 1989. By 1994, every Disney World park had at least one location that served these giant turkey legs.

Liberty Square Market also sells a handful of other items, such as fresh fruit, pickles, hot dogs, chips, and mini snack cheeses. Behind the main stall is a seating area with umbrella-covered seating. This spot can be very busy during the heat of the day and is also a regular spot for people who need a break to sit while the rest of their party rides Haunted Mansion. So, if you plan on getting a snack from this location, you might have to continue walking or head over behind Ye Olde Christmas Shoppe to find additional seating.

A RESTAURANT THAT BRIDGES TWO LANDS

Right on the border of Frontierland and Liberty Square is The Diamond Horseshoe. This sit-down restaurant has some of the most confusing theming as it is technically within the boundaries of Liberty Square but is designed to look like an old western music hall that could be found in a mining town. Perhaps the confusion is fitting for a location that has seen many changes over the years, including drastic changes to the menu and operation. When the saloon-like location opened in 1971, it was a sit-down restaurant that performed Wild West entertainment hosted by Slue Foot Sue and her can-can dancers, along with appearances by a traveling salesman and Pecos Bill. The first version of the show was almost identical to the show that was performed at The Golden Horseshoe restaurant in Disneyland.

After 1986, the show and the menu changed frequently, changing from a sit-down location to a quick-service location, back to a sit-down location, and back to a quick-service location. Eventually, The Diamond Horseshoe stopped serving food altogether and became a meet-and-greet location for characters before closing its doors for five years from 2004–2009. During this time, even though it was technically closed, the restaurant reopened in a limited fashion seasonally to serve sandwiches, chips, and soda. After 2020, The Diamond Horseshoe reopened on a regular basis, serving an all-you-care-to-enjoy meal with two different delicious options. Choose between:

1. **A Frontier Feast:** complete with salad, turkey, pot roast, pork, mashed potatoes, veggies, herb stuffing, and macaroni and cheese, and finished with Ooey Gooey Toffee Cake. (If you think that sounds a lot like the meal served over at Liberty Tree Tavern, that's because it is the same.)
2. **A Cowpoke Platter:** served with salad, Impossible Meatloaf, mashed potatoes, gravy, veggies, and Johnny Appleseed's Warm Apple Cake.

The food is very similar to that of Liberty Tree Tavern, but the restaurant unfortunately does not include any stage entertainment like it used to back in the day. The prices are identical too, making this a great spot to eat if you can't get a reservation at Liberty Tree Tavern and are looking for a very filling meal.

IT'S ALWAYS CHRISTMAS AT THIS SHOPPE

Ye Olde Christmas Shoppe has become a family favorite for securing a personalized ornament—a tangible memory to adorn a holiday tree. You may notice as you walk through the store that there are subtle design changes in each room and on the outside of the building. That's because the location was originally three separate merchandise locations: an antique store, a silversmith, and a perfumery. These three locations were combined into a single store in 1996 and became Ye Olde Christmas Shoppe.

The location celebrates holidays. Any ornament can be personalized here if it was bought at the park or at a Disney resort during your current stay with proof of purchase.

🍴 DON'T LOSE YOUR HEAD OVER THE FOOD AT SLEEPY HOLLOW!

Sleepy Hollow, located just over the bridge as you enter Liberty Square, is a location that people will rush to first thing in the morning. It is one of the only quick-service locations open in the morning, and you can secure Mickey waffles, funnel cakes, and hand-dipped corn dogs here. Any funnel cake and Mickey waffle can be customized for an additional cost, with options like a topping of berries or bananas or a rich hazelnut spread. Whatever your choice, remember that calories don't count on vacation! This spot is busy first thing in the morning— however, by midday and late afternoon, the crowd will often fade. If the line seems long, mobile order to avoid the queue.

Fun fact: This is one of two places in Magic Kingdom where you can find a reference to Halloween all year long. Sleepy Hollow is named after that infamous spooky forest in the short story "The Legend of Sleepy Hollow" by Washington Irving. In the story, Ichabod Crane encounters the Headless Horseman on Halloween night in Sleepy Hollow.

? HOW DID ICHABOD CRANE HELP SAVE DISNEY?

Before the release of *The Adventures of Ichabod and Mr. Toad* in 1949, the Disney studio was facing financial hardship and was releasing anthology films (which are collections of short films on the same theme or topic). *The Adventures of Ichabod and Mr. Toad,* however, would be the last of these "package pictures" for a while.

One of the ways Disney kept costs down during the production of *The Adventures of Ichabod and Mr. Toad* was recycling animation. Existing animation from *The Old Mill* and *The Martins and Coys* shorts was used throughout the film. This is most apparent in the character of Katrina, who was styled to look like the character of Grace Martin from *The Martins and Coys.* These cutbacks saved the studio money, which was then put toward its next feature-length film. That next film went on to become an instant classic and saved Disney Studios from its financial troubles.

Which full-length Disney feature film followed *The Adventures of Ichabod and Mr. Toad* and became a big commercial success?

 GHOSTS ARE GREAT HOSTS!

"Welcome, foolish mortals, to the Haunted Mansion!" One of the most popular attractions in the park, Haunted Mansion was also an opening day attraction at Magic Kingdom. In fact, plans for the Florida Project were well underway during the development and construction of Disneyland's Haunted Mansion attraction, so two of almost every animatronic, prop, display, and gag were created to help speed along the process of bringing the ride to Magic Kingdom. Most of the core storyline pieces are identical, with two notable exceptions that were created for the version at Magic Kingdom: the music room and the library.

Some other notable differences can be found in the functionality of the attraction. For example, the "stretching" room in Disneyland functions as an elevator, taking guests down and under the Disneyland train tracks into the attraction. The same functionality wasn't needed for Magic Kingdom, but the effect was so well received in Disneyland that the concept was brought to Disney World, with the ceiling extending upward to create the stretching effect.

Haunted Mansion is famous for its Imagineering details, and the exterior is no exception. The mansion is strategically placed as a nod to the haunted mansions that often appear in ghost stories on a hill in the outskirts of a town. In Magic Kingdom, the town just so happens to be Liberty Square. To blend in with the architecture of this neighboring colonial village, the exterior is based on the nineteenth-century Dutch Gothic architectural style that was prevalent in the northeastern states.

❓ A NEW ROOM IN AN OLD MANSION

This spooky room was added to the Magic Kingdom's version of the
attraction in 2007 and takes inspiration from an art piece entitled
Relativity and a famous house in California. (Prior to 2007, this portion of the ride was just a darkened black space with large glowing
spiders and webs.)

Which area was added to the Haunted Mansion?

DREADFUL DRAMA

As you enter into the family graveyard portion of the queue for Haunted Mansion, there are five family busts representing the deceased members of the Dread Family. The Dreads were one of the cursed families that supposedly lived in the Haunted Mansion—that is, until they murdered each other in an attempt to seize the family's wealth. But the riddle in this queue area is to find out who killed who. If you want to figure out the riddle, start by reading the plaques on the columns beneath the busts. Find the first one to be murdered and look for clues, both on the busts and on the plaques. When you have figured it out, read on to double-check your answer! Hint: Start by reading Jacob Dread's plaque first.

Figure it out? Let's see how well you did with uncovering the family drama.

★ The first to go was Uncle Jacob, who began hoarding all the family wealth until his relatives found out. His plaque reads, "Greed was the poison he had swallowed. He went first, the others followed. The killer's face he surely knew. Now try to discover who killed who."

★ To the far left you will see Bertie with his pet snake around his neck. Bertie killed Uncle Jacob using the venom from his pet snake (another hint is located on his plaque, which shows a vial). Who killed Bertie? His plaque reads, "Avid hunter and expert shot. In the end that's what he got." This leads to the assumption that Bertie was shot. His killer is to his immediate right: Aunt Florence.

- ★ Aunt Florence was Uncle Jacob's wife and sought vengeance for her late husband. On the top of her plaque is the image of a gun, highlighting the murder weapon. Aunt Florence's plaque reads, "Never did a dishonorable deed. Yet found face down in canary seed." To the right are the last family members, the twins and Cousin Maude. Which one killed Aunt Florence?
- ★ The sour-faced siblings Wellington and Forsythia did it, and placed between their figures is the murder weapon: a bag of bird seed. Their plaque reads, "Departed life while in their beds, with identical bumps on identical heads."
- ★ This leaves Cousin Maude, the final suspect with a hammer icon on the top of her plaque. The family drama ended with her, as her plaque reads, "Our sleeping beauty who never awoke, the night her dreams went up in smoke." This might leave you wondering, who started the fire that took out Cousin Maude? In the end, her own foolishness was her demise. Maude had a habit of using matchsticks as hairpins. If you look in the bun at the back of the bust's head, you will see the three little matchsticks that did her in.

Extra Magic

★

The graves around Haunted Mansion are not real.
This includes the pet cemetery located on the hill to the right of the mansion just past the entrance. The pet cemetery is the final resting place for eight animals: Eric the snake, Maisy the poodle, a monkey, Rover the dog, Whiskers the cat, Jed the cockatoo, Waddle the duck, and J. Thaddeus Toad. The last animal is more commonly known as Mr. Toad from the animated film *The Adventures of Ichabod and Mr. Toad*. Mr. Toad was added to the pet cemetery at Haunted Mansion shortly after Mr. Toad's Wild Ride closed in Fantasyland in 1998 to make way for The Many Adventures of Winnie the Pooh attraction. Mr. Toad's Wild Ride had a mighty fan following, so in honor of this opening day attraction and its passionate fans, Imagineers placed the figure of Mr. Toad at the top of the pet cemetery. His ride may be gone, but he's not forgotten.

🍴 DELICIOUS FOOD AHOY!

Craving a little seafood while in Magic Kingdom? Columbia Harbour House is a quick-service location tucked in the back of Liberty Square, right on the edge of Fantasyland. Here you can find all the flavors of the land and sea. Columbia Harbour House is themed after a colonial New England dining establishment, with model ships, paintings, and maps reminiscent of the age of sailing. While the location is best known for its fried shrimp, lobster roll, and New England clam chowder, you can also find chicken strips, hushpuppies, and French fries if you don't have your sea legs yet. If you are looking for a little peace and quiet with your meal, head upstairs, where there is ample additional seating along with views out on Rivers of America, Liberty Square, and Haunted Mansion.

⚙ SEND US A MESSAGE FROM SOMEWHERE BEYOND!

Memento Mori is a well-known gift shop for all things Haunted Mansion. The shop pays tribute to one of the most famous apparitions in the attraction: Madame Leota. While Madame Leota appears in the séance room of the attraction around the world, her lore and backstory are most unique in Magic Kingdom. In 2002, the medium was given a headstone near the entrance of the attraction, where every few moments her eyes will open and look around at guests in the queue. Her tombstone reads, "Dear sweet Leota, beloved by all. In regions beyond now, but having a ball."

Leota is truly beloved as a character, so much so that in 2014, The Yankee Trader store that used to be here was transformed into Memento Mori. In the backstory of the gift shop, this quaint little house was once the humble abode of Madame Leota herself. To tie in with the theming of Liberty Square, the lore is that Madame Leota fled Massachusetts at the beginning of the Salem witch trials and found friends and solace with the Gracey household, the original owners of Haunted Mansion. Her little home and shop were built just off the edge of Gracey Manor. While Madame Leota has passed away, her collection of artifacts can still be found on the top of shelves, along with a large portrait of how she appeared in her "corruptible mortal state."

CHAPTER 6

Fantasyland

With a little faith, trust, and sprinkling of pixie dust, you are transported to the magical world of Fantasyland! When Disney fans think of Magic Kingdom, they often picture Fantasyland first. This is likely because Walt Disney imagined Fantasyland as the place for guests to step directly into the films of Disney—where characters and creations from the films would come to life almost magically.

This area has seen some of the biggest changes within Magic Kingdom over the years, with rides, entertainment, and food coming and going. These changes have also led to an expansion of the area. In 2012, Disney added a little over 26 acres to Fantasyland, which brought the Storybook Circus and Enchanted Forest areas to life. Fantasyland is now broken up into three sections: Enchanted Forest, Castle Courtyard, and Storybook Circus. You won't see these three sections labeled on a map, but you can tell they exist because of subtle park design. While Storybook Circus has the strongest visual identity, the towers and turrets behind Cinderella Castle are a more subtle way that Imagineers established the boundary between the Castle Courtyard and Enchanted Forest areas. These visual boundaries also play into the storytelling for Fantasyland by reinforcing that the castles of Ariel and Prince Eric, Belle and Beast, and Cinderella and Prince Charming are all located in distinct, neighboring kingdoms instead of sharing property.

Beyond Disney princesses, Fantasyland is also the home of many other classic characters, like Peter Pan, Anastasia and Drizella, Pinocchio, Winnie the Pooh, and many more! Scattered throughout the land are also multiple dining options, including upscale sit-down options like Cinderella's Royal Table and Be Our Guest Restaurant, as well as simple quick-service locations like Pinocchio Village Haus and Gaston's Tavern. Now, enough fantasizing—let's head through Fantasyland!

YOU KNOW THE WORDS TO THIS SONG

Love it or hate it, "it's a small world" is one of the most renowned attractions in Disney history. The attraction debuted at the 1964 World's Fair and was sponsored by Pepsi-Cola; "it's a small world" was overwhelmingly popular, and after the conclusion of the World's Fair, Disney relocated the attraction to Disneyland's Fantasyland to continue to delight guests of all ages. Shortly thereafter, a version of the attraction was planned for Magic Kingdom as an opening day attraction.

Over the years, a tradition of sorts was created. In the water surrounding the loading area of the attraction, thousands of coins can be seen below. Guests take their spare change and make a wish just as they would at a wishing well. When it comes time to clean the attraction,

Cast Members vacuum out the coins, count them, and donate the total to local children's charities.

So, what is it about this attraction that captivates guests? Is it the song? The bright and cheerful colors? Hypnotic puppeteering? While the song and colors certainly have a hand in the popularity of "it's a small world" (although not a hypnotic one!), the reality is that the "propulsion" style of attraction played the largest role in cementing the ride as a family favorite.

The first attraction to use the propulsion system, "it's a small world" paved the way for other water attractions in later years, like Tiana's Bayou Adventure and Pirates of the Caribbean! The unique, high-capacity boat flume system (in other words, flowing water that makes the boats go!) is perfect for families and children of all ages. The large boats allow entire families to experience the magic of an attraction together and also ensure that the ride has significant capacity for even the largest crowds to enjoy "the happiest cruise that ever sailed."

TAKE FLIGHT WITH PETER PAN!

"Come on, everybody! Here we go! Off to Never Land!" Don't miss this exciting chance to fly with Peter. Disney's animated take on the story of the boy who never grows up is one of the most popular Disney stories to this day. Inspired by the 1953 film *Peter Pan*, Peter Pan's Flight lets you soar off to Never Land aboard your very own pixie dust–powered pirate ship. The attraction's unique overhead rail system creates the illusion of flight as you take to the sky through classic scenes from the movie, including the Darlings' bedroom, London from above, the Mermaid Lagoon, and Captain Hook's ship. Peter Pan's Flight is considered an opening day attraction at Magic Kingdom; however, the ride was delayed in opening for two days and technically opened on October 3, 1971.

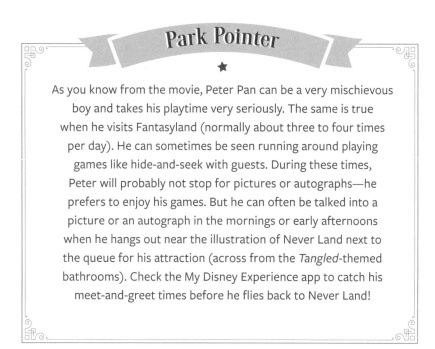

Park Pointer

★

As you know from the movie, Peter Pan can be a very mischievous boy and takes his playtime very seriously. The same is true when he visits Fantasyland (normally about three to four times per day). He can sometimes be seen running around playing games like hide-and-seek with guests. During these times, Peter will probably not stop for pictures or autographs—he prefers to enjoy his games. But he can often be talked into a picture or an autograph in the mornings or early afternoons when he hangs out near the illustration of Never Land next to the queue for his attraction (across from the *Tangled*-themed bathrooms). Check the My Disney Experience app to catch his meet-and-greet times before he flies back to Never Land!

? NEVER LAND IS WORTH THE WAIT

Peter Pan's Flight always seems to have a long line of guests waiting to climb aboard. Is it because Tick-Tock the Crocodile ate the clock? The average queue time for this attraction ranges between forty and sixty minutes, but can be much longer at peak times. The long waits and enduring popularity of Peter Pan is one of the main reasons that the attraction received an update in 2015 to extend the queue area. With the extension, there is more room for guests to wait inside in themed rooms and escape the Florida sun in air-conditioning!

Why is the line always long for Peter Pan's Flight?

- **A.** It's so popular.
- **B.** The attraction moves slowly.
- **C.** It has a low ride capacity.

 ## STARRY NIGHT

When Peter Pan bursts into the room of the Darling children, it doesn't take long before they learn that they can fly too (with a little pixie dust). Soon they are eager to head off to Never Land!

In the film, Peter gives the Darling children very specific instructions for how to find Never Land—can you remember them? How do you find Never Land in the night sky?

- **A.** "First star to the right, until you find the light."
- **B.** "Second star to the left, and straight on till evening."
- **C.** "Second star to the right, and straight on till morning."

 ## 4D FUN!

Mickey's PhilharMagic is a fabulously fun musical journey in 4D! In the attraction, Donald Duck steals the show (literally) as you follow his journey to capture Mickey's sorcerer hat. Mickey's PhilharMagic opened in 2003 and pays homage to the original attraction that was housed in the theater: The Mickey Mouse Revue. In the original attraction, maestro Mickey leads an Audio-Animatronic band through magical musical moments in classic Disney animated films. Famous Disney characters would appear in animatronic form to sing to the guests. In Mickey's PhilharMagic, the journey takes an exciting turn as the guests are transported into the sights, sensations, and even smells of this immersive adventure through classic Disney and Pixar films. With Donald Duck in charge, what could go wrong?

❓ WHO DOES FIGARO BELONG TO, ANYWAY?

Most people do a double take when they see Figaro. This cat from *Pinocchio* looks a lot like Minnie Mouse's pet cat. That's because these cats are one and the same! Figaro belongs to both Geppetto and Minnie. So how did this come about? While creating the character of Figaro during the animation for *Pinocchio,* Walt Disney became attached to the character. That adorable face was too hard to resist, and Walt wanted to find another way to utilize the character outside of the movie. The easiest way to achieve this was to give the cat to Minnie Mouse. Figaro would go on to appear in multiple shorts as one of Minnie's pets and can still be seen in this role today!

What color cat is Figaro?

- **A.** Black and white
- **B.** Brown
- **C.** White

DUAL-NATIONALITY AND DELICIOUS

Pinocchio Village Haus can be a slightly confusing location: vaguely German architecture with Italian food inside? The reason for this contradiction is found in the story of *Pinocchio* itself. The original story was written by an Italian author and likely set in northern Italy, but one of the leading animators in the Disney film used a Bavarian town as inspiration for the creation of Pinocchio's village. Both of these factors played heavily into the storytelling of Pinocchio Village Haus.

Whatever the reason for the design, inside you will find flatbread pizzas, breadsticks, and Caesar salads. Pepperoni or cheese flatbread is a tried-and-true classic, but if you're looking for something a little more exciting, try one of the specialty flatbreads or seasonal offerings. Another important note: While most locations across Disney World property are happy to provide options to guests with dietary or allergy restrictions, this location is especially accommodating! You can get flatbreads with vegan cheese, for example, or find choices that suit those with allergies to sesame, soy, peanut/tree nut, dairy, or gluten. Simply check with a Cast Member to see what options are available.

Extra Magic

★

Hidden inside the dining room of Pinocchio Village Haus to the left of the entrance is a stained-glass window with an image of the Blue Fairy from the movie *Pinocchio*, with script that reads, "You deserve to have your wish come true." Below this image is a small desk with a book. This is a wish book where you can leave a little note to the Blue Fairy with your wishes and heart's desires. What a perfect magical moment hidden within the restaurant!

 DINE WITH THE PRINCESSES

Every little prince and princess has dreamed of dining in a real castle. At Cinderella's Royal Table, you can make that dream come true! Here you'll dine like royalty and get to meet royalty too. The location is open for breakfast, lunch, and dinner and serves a three-course meal. The dining room for Cinderella's Royal Table overlooks Prince Charming Regal Carrousel and the Castle Courtyard area of Fantasyland.

Inside, Cinderella will greet you on arrival before you are ushered upstairs to the dining room. There you'll have the chance to meet some of the visiting royalty, such as Princess Ariel, Princess Snow White,

Princess Aurora, and Princess Jasmine. There is also the occasional guest appearance by other adventurous princesses, like Merida. A fun fact you may notice while dining: There are coats of arms and family crests dotted throughout the castle. These represent the families of Imagineers and other people important to the creation of Magic Kingdom.

CHOOSE YOUR STEED AND SPIN THROUGH FANTASYLAND!

Located in the heart of Fantasyland is Prince Charming Regal Carrousel. This beautiful opening day attraction is actually older than the park itself. The carousel was originally built in 1917 by the Philadelphia Toboggan Company, one of the most prestigious carousel manufacturers of its time. Before making its way to Magic Kingdom, the carousel was known as the Liberty Carrousel at Olympic Park, in Maplewood, New Jersey, and had a patriotic theme.

Though the overall patriotic color scheme is now gone, nods to the carousel's heritage are still hidden on the rounding boards. Next to the images telling Cinderella's story, you will see images of Lady Liberty leaning on a shield. She is no longer painted red, white, and blue, but rather pink and blue to fit the theme of Fantasyland. Another detail reminiscent of the patriotic theme are the stars, stripes, and shields found on many of the carousel's horses. The single sleigh on the carousel is the only one left out of an original four, and it depicts Lady Liberty riding in a chariot accompanied by the American bald eagle.

? ALL THE PRINCE'S HORSES

How many horses are on Prince Charming Regal Carrousel?

- **A.** 80
- **B.** 65
- **C.** 90

Extra Magic

★

While all the horses on Prince Charming Regal Carrousel might look alike to you, there is one that stands out to Cast Members as "Cinderella's horse." Do you know which one it is? Look in the second ring from the outside for the horse with gems on its saddle and flowers in its mane. It is also the only horse with a gold bow in its tail. According to Cast Members, this horse belongs to the princess herself. If you run into Cinderella and ask her which horse is hers, she might tell you that they are all her favorites and that she couldn't possibly pick just one.

You may have noticed a family crest on the exterior of Cinderella Castle. It is prominently displayed on both the front and the back of the castle, just above the tunnel entrance, as well as on the front turrets facing out toward Main Street U.S.A. This family crest doesn't belong to the famous princess; rather, it is the crest of the Disney family. There are a couple variations of the family crest. The one used here has three lions on the center shield with a helmet above and an additional lion placed on top of the helmet. The same crest can also be found on Sleeping Beauty Castle in Disneyland, connecting the castles coast-to-coast.

ROYAL TREASURE

Sir Mickey's shop is the place in Fantasyland to find all the treasures inspired by Disney royalty. Princess dresses, costumes, and accessories can all be found here. The theme of the little cottage played into the Imagineering of this area of Fantasyland by referencing two Mickey Mouse short films:

1. The 1938 short *Brave Little Tailor* is represented by Mickey's sewing supplies (which are hidden behind the registers and on some of the upper shelves and by Mickey himself, in his tailor costume from the film).

2. The other film referenced is the 1947 short *Mickey and the Beanstalk*, as evidenced by the beanstalk on the outside of the cottage with vines and leaves breaking through the ceiling and walls into the shop. Inside, Willie the Giant can also be seen peering in, trying to find Mickey.

 **FRIAR FARE**

Hidden just to the right of Prince Charming Regal Carrousel toward Seven Dwarfs Mine Train is a quick-service dining location named The Friar's Nook. This location is inspired by the character of Friar Tuck from the 1973 animated Disney movie *Robin Hood*. The nook is appropriately named, since it's a cozy spot to grab a quick bite.

The Friar's Nook is one of the few locations in Magic Kingdom that is open early for breakfast and serves items like sausage, cheddar, and egg bagels, and cheddar, bacon, and ranch tots. This location's lunch menu has changed over the years, but it typically carries park favorites like hot dogs, macaroni and cheese, and seasonal snacks.

ONCE UPON A SUNDAE

Immediately to the right of The Friar's Nook is Storybook Treats, a quick-service location that features sweets only. In recent years this location has become popular thanks to its seasonal and limited-edition soft serve ice cream collection. Two options that have become popular mainstays are the Rapunzel Sundae and the Aurora Cone. Both combine Dole Whip and soft serve ice cream into a happily-ever-after treat that will be sure to hit the spot. If you prefer a classic ending to your storybook day, never fear! Traditional soft serve, sundaes, and floats are on the menu as well.

IS THERE SOMETHING THERE THAT WASN'T THERE BEFORE?

You may have passed by Enchanted Tales with Belle without even noticing it or assuming that it was nothing more than a standard Disney princesses meet-and-greet location. There is so much more! Enchanted Tales with Belle is one of the most immersive ways to meet a Disney character. Inside you'll step into Belle's childhood cottage and make your way to her father's workshop. Among Maurice's tools and current projects, you'll find the enchanted mirror that Beast gave to Belle as a wedding gift. With the help of some magic words, the mirror comes to life and transports you to the past, where Belle and Beast fell in love. You will encounter other enchanted characters, and members of the audience may be picked to help retell Belle's love story. This experience is definitely not one to miss for guests of all ages!

The separation of the areas in Fantasyland (Enchanted Forest, Castle Courtyard, and Storybook Circus) can be seen in the Cast Member costumes. Castle Courtyard Cast Members wear blues, whites, pinks, and purples, while Cast Members wearing greens, yellows, and browns are Enchanted Forest Cast. These small details play an important role immersing guests in the world of magic, princesses, and dreams just as Walt imagined!

A DINNER HERE IS NEVER SECOND-BEST

Hidden away in the deepest edge of the Enchanted Forest area of Fantasyland sits Beast's castle, which is home to Be Our Guest Restaurant. Here you are invited to experience a "tale as old as time" in an immersive fine dining setting. The meal is served in three courses, each with French flair. There are three dining areas where you can enjoy your meal that immerse you in different parts of the movie.

★ **The West Wing:** This is Beast's study in the fearsome west wing of the castle, where you will be surrounded by torn and tattered remnants of large tapestries. Highlighted in the corner of the room is the legendary rose that floats under a glass canopy, waiting for the spell to be broken. As each petal falls, lightning flashes and the roll of thunder echoes through the room. You might also notice that the torn portrait of the prince transforms into an image of his beastly form as the petal falls.

* **The Grand Ballroom:** The ballroom is the largest room and features a high, domed ceiling and magnificent glass windows overlooking a diorama-style snowy mountain scene. The ceiling above is decorated with cherubs surrounding the opulent chandeliers that truly give the effect of stepping into the film's iconic ballroom scene.
* **The Rose Gallery:** This quaint room isn't based on any specific room from Beast's castle seen in the film. A gallery of artwork depicting fond moments Belle had with Beast and her friends in the castle hangs on the walls, and a giant, 7-foot-tall music box stands in the middle, highlighting Belle and Beast dancing.

No matter which room you dine in, Be Our Guest is a fun and immersive dining experience. Keep an eye out for Beast himself as he strolls through the dining rooms to greet his guests. As a reminder, this is a three-course meal, but make sure you leave enough room for dessert. Try the Grey Stuff (it's delicious!).

NO ONE BAKES CINNAMON ROLLS LIKE GASTON

The guy you love to hate, Gaston, has his own tavern in Fantasyland. Resembling the iconic tavern scene from *Beauty and the Beast*, this location makes it feel as though you are stepping in to grab a drink with the local town celebrity. Some of the immersive details include Gaston's hunting trophies on the walls, his chair in the corner next to the fireplace, and an oversized portrait of himself above the mantel.

Gaston's Tavern serves a family-friendly brew in the form of a signature nonalcoholic drink called LeFou's Brew. Served cold, the drink is a frozen apple juice mixture with hints of marshmallow topped with a passion fruit–mango foam and makes for a wonderful respite in the summer's heat. The tavern also serves cinnamon rolls, which are widely regarded as some of the best baked goods on Disney property. You can also sample the fabled Grey Stuff referenced in *Beauty and the Beast* here in cupcake form. No one serves sweet treats like Gaston!

Extra Magic

★

Have you ever seen the little door located right behind Bonjour! Village Gifts? This door has become very popular on social media in the past several years. You can find it if you look down and to the left coming out of the restrooms near Bonjour Gifts. Many have wondered what purpose this little door serves. Is it for storage? Is there a fire hydrant hidden behind it? The truth is that it is a construction error. If you look at the ground in front of the door, you'll notice that the edge of the wall is within centimeters of a manhole cover. If the wall was completely straight and the door was not there, the wall would have covered the manhole. The easiest way to fix this was to make it fun, so Disney cut out the shape of a small door the same width as the manhole and set it into the wall just far back enough that the cover could still be accessed. It's a bit of Disney magic to make a seemingly mundane mistake become magical.

❓ PORTRAIT OF A CAST MEMBER

When Disney opened the Fantasyland expansion in 2012, Phil Holmes was Vice President of Magic Kingdom. Phil got his start with Disney as an opening day Cast Member at Haunted Mansion, then worked his way up the ranks. In 2012, he was celebrating forty years with the company. To honor his hard work, Disney commemorated a very special portrait of Phil and placed it in Fantasyland. In this portrait, there are a few hidden references, including a gold ring on Phil's hand with the number 40 on it as well as a gold statue of Donald Duck on the shelf behind him. (A gold Donald Duck statue is the award typically presented to Cast Members celebrating forty years of service.) There are several other hidden references to his accomplishments during his time at Magic Kingdom.

Like Phil, Cast Members around the world receive recognition for the number of years they have worked for the Disney company. These are called service awards. Cast Members start receiving their service awards after their one-year anniversary with the company, when they receive a pin of Mickey dressed as Steamboat Willie that can be added to their name tags. They then receive a new pin and award every five years afterward. As the Disney company grows, there are some Cast Members that have been with the company for more than sixty years! There are now more than a dozen service awards.

Can you match which character is associated with these award years?

CHARACTER	YEARS OF SERVICE
Pluto	20
Tinker Bell	10
Simba	5
TaDa Mickey	25

 EVER WANTED TO BE PART OF THAT WORLD?

Tucked away in the seaside caves next to Prince Eric's castle is an attraction full of Disney Imagineering. Step into the story of Princess Ariel in the Under the Sea—Journey of The Little Mermaid attraction. A well-designed queue will have you scanning the walls for some of Ariel's "gadgets and gizmos" as Scuttle the seagull and his crab pals highlight some of their favorite human treasures. Once inside, you hop aboard your personal clamshell transport into a world "under the sea" as you revisit some of the most beloved scenes from Disney's 1989 film *The Little Mermaid*. As you enter into Ursula's lair, you'll see one of the most impressive animatronics on Disney property, as the sea witch sings "Poor Unfortunate Souls." This animatronic stands over 7½ feet tall, with her tentacles stretching 12 feet wide. Don't worry, your clamshell whisks you away before she can steal your voice! Now you'll follow the love story of Princess Ariel and Prince Eric as they foil Ursula's plans and live happily ever after. By the end of the ride, you'll be singing along as though you *are* part of that world!

Park Pointer

★

While there are a number of places you *could* bump into royalty during your time in Fantasyland, there are also a few spots where you can wait in line to make sure you meet some of the most beloved princesses. Near Prince Charming Regal Carrousel is Princess Fairytale Hall, with two separate queues for an audience with a royal. One is for Princess Cinderella, while the other is for Princess Tiana. Each princess is also joined by an additional surprise princess that varies day by day (princesses are very busy). Another location to meet a princess is near Under the Sea—Journey of The Little Mermaid in Ariel's Grotto. Here you can meet with Ariel in her mermaid form.

ALL IN A DAY'S WORK

Heigh-ho, heigh-ho! It's off to Seven Dwarfs Mine Train we go! Fantasyland's family-friendly coaster takes you on a high-speed journey with the seven dwarfs from *Snow White* into the diamond mines. The ride is nearly three minutes of fun as you experience both a roller coaster–type ride and a traditional Disney "dark ride." Dark rides refer to attractions that use a controlled mixture of lighting, sound, and other effects to transport the riders through multiple narrative scenes. In Seven Dwarfs Mine Train, this section of the ride occurs as you enter the mine. This combination of attraction styles is a unique feature of this ride. Another special aspect is that the mine cars can be swung side to side by their occupants. Next time you are moving through the mine, try coordinating your swinging with everyone in your car to the timing of the music to see this feature in action! This attraction is fun for all ages and very popular, so be prepared to wait for this adventure into the mines.

Luckily, the queue for Seven Dwarfs Mine Train is an adventure in itself, so the wait is entertaining! As you weave around a forest-like setting into the entrance of the diamond mine, you will see some written notes along the way. These notes are clues from the dwarfs on how to best engage with the interactive elements of the queue. One of the best experiences in the line can only be achieved with the help of some friends. After entering the mine, you will come across some barrels of diamonds as the line loops back on itself. There are seven barrels that can spin. As each barrel spins faster and faster, a dancing dwarf will appear on the ceiling. If you can get all seven barrels spinning fast enough with each dwarf dancing, Snow White herself will appear on the ceiling in the center and will twirl and dance around like in the movie! Enlist the help of other guests in the queue to help get all the barrels spinning to see this amazing element.

When is the best time to try to catch a ride into the mines? There isn't an answer that will guarantee a shorter time, but two times of the day generally have shorter waits. The first is when the park opens in the morning, so head to the attraction as early as you possibly can. Check your reservation to see if your hotel includes Early Theme Park Entry first thing on select mornings. Another option is to try during the evening fireworks show. Typically, the wait times will drop as soon as the fireworks start going off; plus, riding at night makes the experience even more thrilling!

❓ ROYAL KNOWLEDGE

Let's do a little matching game and test your knowledge of Cinderella Castle.

Match each statement to the correct answer:

The castle was decorated as a pink birthday cake.	False
The castle has no bricks in it.	False
The castle retracts into the basement in case of hurricanes.	True
There is a suite in the castle that you can reserve.	True

❓ MAGICAL MOSAICS

Located in the heart of Cinderella Castle is a breezeway with five mosaic murals that tell the story of Cinderella. These beautiful artworks are composed of hand-cut glass pieces. Each of the panels is approximately 15' × 10' and was installed or created on-site during the construction of Magic Kingdom. The panels were designed by Dorothea Redmond and were brought to life by mosaicist Hanns-Joachim Scharff. These mosaics contain silver, gold, and Italian glass. Truly artwork fit for a princess!

How many pieces of Italian glass were used in creating the mosaics for Cinderella Castle?

A. 10,000

B. 500,000

C. 250,000

D. Over 1 million

 # A JOURNEY THROUGH HUNDRED-ACRE WOOD

Jump aboard a giant Hunny Pot for a wild ride through Hundred-Acre Wood in The Many Adventures of Winnie the Pooh! The attraction is named after the 1977 Winnie the Pooh movie of the same name. The attraction encompasses all three of the stories that are represented in the movie, as well as a fourth storyline from *Winnie the Pooh and a Day for Eeyore*, which was added to *The Many Adventures of Winnie the Pooh* in 1983 when the film was rereleased in movie theaters. The attraction opened in Magic Kingdom in 1999 during the height of the Winnie the Pooh merchandise craze. This family-friendly attraction was created to immerse guests in the story of everyone's favorite silly ol' bear.

The Many Adventures of Winnie the Pooh replaced the slightly scarier attraction Mr. Toad's Wild Ride. A few references to the former attraction are tucked away and can be seen on the ride. For example, in Owl's fallen house on the left side as you move through the attraction, there is a framed picture of Mr. Toad handing the deed to the house to Owl. On the right side at nearly the same spot is a picture of Mr. Toad's friend Moley next to Winnie the Pooh.

The Many Adventures of Winnie the Pooh is still just as thrilling as the ride it replaced, as your Hunny Pot bounces along with Tigger, weaves through Heffalumps and Woozles, and bobs down the river past Pooh Bear's house. This ride also has a great interactive queue for little ones, with a re-creation of Eeyore's house, tiles to jump to get gophers out of Rabbit's Garden, and walls of dripping honey with images of Pooh Bear's friends hidden underneath.

Extra Magic

★

Located at the entrance to The Many Adventures of Winnie the Pooh is a large tree that is a re-creation of Pooh Bear's house. It also has the sign for the attraction hanging from its branches. This tree was formerly located across the path, where the queue for Seven Dwarfs Mine Train is today, but was moved to its current location during the construction of Seven Dwarfs Mine Train and added to the interactive queue expansion in the Adventures of Pooh queue. The tree was originally part of a play space that opened in 2005 called Pooh's Playful Spot. The play space was placed over the site of the closed 20,000 Leagues Under the Sea: Submarine Voyage attraction. To pay homage to this opening day water-based attraction, an image of Captain Nemo's *Nautilus* submarine was carved inside the tree above the larger entrance. Be sure to pop in and see if you can find this tiny impression of the *Nautilus*.

 TO SPIN OR NOT TO SPIN

A classic from opening day, Mad Tea Party was designed to match its sibling attraction on the West Coast in Disneyland, with every detail identical—down to its lack of a roof. This was an oversight on the part of Imagineers unaccustomed to the Florida summer heat and summer rain showers. The installation of a roof was one of the first major attraction updates made, occurring less than two years after Magic Kingdom opened. Today, Mad Tea Party sits under a beautiful canopy of oak trees as well as a roof designed to provide shade from the hot sun.

The speed of the teacup spin is controlled by the guests riding in the car. The attraction consists of one giant turntable that rotates counterclockwise, with three smaller turntables rotating clockwise on top. On each of the smaller turntables are six teacups that are able to be spun clockwise at your desired speed. Communication is key here. Decide with your party if you will spin or not and how hard. Refrain from eating before riding and hold on to your teacup!

Park Pointer

★

In recent years, the Mad Tea Party attraction has received a holiday overlay for Mickey's Not-So-Scary Halloween Party and Mickey's Very Merry Christmas Party dates. During the Halloween overlay, ghostly music, lighting effects, and an eerie mist make for a spooky spin. During the Christmas party, guests see red and green lights accompanied by holiday music fit for Wonderland.

 THE CAT'S MEOW

No trip to Wonderland would be complete without a visit from Cheshire Cat! In Fantasyland, you can stop by Cheshire Café for a sweet snack inspired by this character. Known for its berry slushies and pastries, this food kiosk has also recently become a test location for select seasonal offerings. The one constant on the menu is the Cheshire Cat Tail: a twisted pastry filled with chocolate and decorated with pink and purple icing stripes to match the famous cat.

 COME FLY WITH ME!

Come one, come all, to see the eighth wonder of the world: Dumbo the Flying Elephant! This attraction is synonymous with classic Disney rides and can be found at Disney locations around the world in Anaheim, Tokyo, Paris, Hong Kong, Shanghai, and of course at Magic Kingdom. Due to the popularity of the original attraction in Disneyland, an identical version was brought to Magic Kingdom and was at first located behind Cinderella Castle near Prince Charming Regal Carrousel.

The attraction has been updated many times over the years, but the biggest change came in 2012 with the opening of the Storybook Circus area. Dumbo the Flying Elephant was moved, updated, and doubled in size! The attraction now includes two ride structures that sit side by side. This makes this version of Dumbo the Flying Elephant the largest in the world and also gives the ride on the left as you enter the unique distinction as the only Dumbo attraction to rotate counterclockwise. This was also one of the first queues to also include a playground waiting area; here, little ones could run around under the big top while waiting for their turn to fly. Grab your magic feather, and let's soar with Dumbo!

GOOFING WITH THE GREAT GOOFINI

Goofy has always been a bit of a daredevil, and here at Storybook Circus he has become the death-defying stuntperson of the circus in The Barnstormer attraction! On this junior roller coaster, guests join Goofy (also known as The Great Goofini) in his stage act as he performs his aerial stunt show. The height requirement for this ride is only 35 inches, so it caters to families with preschool-age daredevils who are ready to try their first big-kid ride. Guests board a little airplane that swoops down into the barnyard on this sixty-three-second ride. Around the queue area you will see posters of some of Goofy's other daredevil attempts.

NUMBERS, NUMBERS, WHAT DO THEY MEAN?

Located in the center of Storybook Circus is the little blue train that brings the circus into town: Casey Jr.! His train cars are full of Dumbo's animal friends, and they've caused quite a splash—Casey Jr. Splash 'N' Soak Station, to be exact. There are four train cars with various animals spraying water. On the back of each of these cars are the numbers 71, 82, 89, 98.

What do the numbers on the train cars represent? (No, these are not the winning lottery numbers.)

🍴 SNACKS UNDER THE BIG TOP

Located within Big Top Souvenirs, directly across from Dumbo the Flying Elephant attraction, is a merchandise store that also sells confectionery goods in the center ring. This is a great location to get a sweet treat for a pick-me-up in the back of the park. With an offering of seasonally rotating snacks, crispy rice cereal treats, caramel apples, and cotton candy, you will be able to find anything you could need for a trip to the circus! If you find yourself here on a hot day, don't miss the Goofy Glacier machine for a refreshing slushy drink. These drinks come in various flavors, and you can also mix and match to create a custom flavor.

Extra Magic

★

Looking for some fabulous photos with four famous friends? Then step right up and visit Pete's Silly Sideshow! Here you can meet Minnie Mouse, Daisy Duck, Donald Duck, and Goofy under the big top as they prepare for their circus acts. Minnie Magnifique appears with her team of pirouetting Parisian poodles. Daisy is dressed as Madame Daisy Fortuna and is ready to look in her crystal ball to read your future. Donald is known as The Astounding Donaldo, the master snake charmer. Goofy appears as his daredevil persona, The Great Goofini! These outfits are exclusive to this meet-and-greet spot if you're looking to meet these fabulous four.

CHAPTER 7

Tomorrowland

Rockets fly overhead and far-away galaxies are just a quick transit ride away in the world of Tomorrowland! This isn't a world of science fiction; it's a land dedicated to the question "What if?" When Walt Disney originally conceived the idea of Tomorrowland for Disneyland, he imagined a place that would inspire children with hope, optimism, and a sense of wonder for the future. Tomorrowland opened in Disneyland as a showcase and celebration of technology and a vision of the future through the lens of the 1950s and 1960s. The same vision was brought to Magic Kingdom's Tomorrowland, but it took several years for Disney to add enough attractions to the land to give it a sense of completion!

When Magic Kingdom opened in 1971, only two attractions were available in Tomorrowland: Skyway's Tomorrowland station and Grand Prix Raceway (now known as Tomorrowland

Speedway). After additional attractions were added, Tomorrowland would stay largely the same from 1975–1994. One of the problems with theming an area focused on futuristic technology is that the future becomes the past very quickly! What was considered ground-breaking technology in the 1950s had become obsolete by the time Tomorrowland in Magic Kingdom was up and running. In 1994, Disney redesigned Tomorrowland into New Tomorrowland, tweaking the theming slightly to emphasize a "What if?" vision for the future. Instead of a world of the future, Tomorrowland imagines a world of what *could be*. What if monsters and humans worked together to create cities powered by laughs? What if going to another planet was as easy as catching a train?

While attractions and aesthetics in Tomorrowland have changed over the years, the core message of the land has remained constantly focused on the vision that tomorrow can be better than today. Just like the future itself, Tomorrowland will keep changing, developing, and moving forward toward a great, big beautiful tomorrow!

"THERE ARE WINNERS AND THERE ARE LOSERS. WHO ARE YOU?"

Enter the Grid and launch into a high-speed cyber race in the world of TRON Lightcycle / Run! You'll join Team Blue and race a Lightcycle against three other teams through a series of energy gates to attempt to claim victory. With a launch speed of just under 60 miles per hour, this ride is not for the faint of heart! One of the most unique aspects of the attraction is the ride vehicle. Guests board the vehicle similarly to a motorcycle, straddling the seat with calf and back restraints sliding into place for security. Because of the intensity of this attraction and the shape of the ride vehicle, you must place your personal items in a locker before entering the load area. If you are unable to board the Lightcycle for any reason, an alternate vehicle is available with a more typical seating configuration. You can try the Lightcycle before entering the ride on several demo vehicles located next to the outdoor queue. Get ready to blast through this digital frontier in Tomorrowland!

Park Pointer

★

Did you know there is a pathway connecting the back of Storybook Circus and Tomorrowland? Most people don't even know this path exists, hence why most think it's a secret. To find it, head past the entrance of The Barnstormer attraction queue. The beginning of the path is nestled between the track for the train and the queue for the attraction. The path will wind you toward the back of Tomorrowland, where a large sign welcomes you into the land. You proceed under the ramp that leads up into TRON Lightcycle / Run. This path is a great way to avoid the thick crowds at the intersection between Fantasyland and Tomorrowland.

A FIRST-OF-ITS-KIND SPACEPORT

One of the most iconic features of the skyline of Magic Kingdom is Space Mountain! The towering pavilion contains a roller coaster that operates in the darkness of space as you whiz past stars and planets in your own rocket ship.

The concept of a roller coaster ride that takes place in the dark had never been done before Walt Disney and Imagineer John Hench conceived what would go on to become Space Mountain. Walt's passion for this project was put on pause because of the 1964 World's Fair, and by the time the project could be restarted, Walt had passed away. The project was not forgotten, although it took another eight years after Walt's passing for the technology, location, and finances to catch up to his dream.

Opening in 1975, this ride was the first roller coaster–type attraction built in Magic Kingdom. The track design was modeled after that of Matterhorn Bobsleds, an attraction that opened in Disneyland in 1959, but the iconic exterior was Hench's original design. A version of this classic attraction can be found in almost every Disney park around the world!

❓ THE SPEED OF SPACE

Blasting through space is quite the ride! As you shoot though the stars, you feel like you are traveling at light speed to weave past planets. While there are no major drops, there are some quick ups and downs and some sharp banking. Given that the ride takes place in the dark, the sound effects and movements give many guests the impression of supersonic speed!

Can you guess what max speed is reached on Space Mountain?

- **A.** 28 mph
- **B.** 42 mph
- **C.** 60 mph

A GREAT, BIG BEAUTIFUL TOMORROW

"A great, big beautiful tomorrow" is the theme of the classic attraction Walt Disney's Carousel of Progress. The attraction was originally created under the name Progressland and debuted at the 1964 New York World's Fair. The rotating theater takes you through the twentieth century, highlighting the advancement of technology in America beginning in the early 1900s.

The attraction itself has been on quite an impressive journey! After groundbreaking success at the World's Fair in New York City, the attraction was dismantled and relocated nearly 3,000 miles away in Disneyland in California. The attraction was renamed Carousel of Progress at this time. In the lead-up to the opening of Magic Kingdom, it was decided that Tomorrowland needed more attractions, and Carousel of Progress was dismantled once again to make its way back to the East Coast. The attraction opened in Magic Kingdom in 1975 as Walt Disney's Carousel of Progress. Since then, this show has become one of the longest-running stage shows in American history. The air-conditioned theater is a great way to beat the Florida heat, and you will likely leave wondering what new technology we will develop next—which is what Walt himself would have wanted!

Extra Magic

★

In Walt Disney's Carousel of Progress, two fun Easter eggs are located in the Christmas scene! The first one can be found on the jacket of the son, James. The emblem on his jacket is the original concept logo for Mineral King Ski Resort—a Disney ski lodge that never came to fruition (check out Chapter 4 and the Extra Magic sidebar about the Country Bear Musical Jamboree band for more details on this project). The second Easter egg is on the slippers of James and his sister, Patricia. On their slippers are images of reindeer with their tongues hanging out. These reindeer designs first appeared as the Silly Reindeer character in Disneyland's 1961 Christmas parade. James's and Patricia's costumes were brought to Magic Kingdom and remained part of the holiday season celebrations until they were updated in the 2010s. The slippers are a great homage to Disney's holiday history!

🍴 DINNER AND A SHOW

Opening in 1994, Cosmic Ray's Starlight Café is the largest quick-service location in Magic Kingdom. The location dishes up burgers, chicken sandwiches, salads, and a whole lot of French fries. If you are looking for a classic theme park burger, look no further than Cosmic Ray's bacon cheeseburger! Recently, the location's menu has also seen some seasonal burgers and special event items. In recent years, Cosmic Ray's has tested some pretty unusual burgers that almost seem . . . alien—like the Angus Pizza Burger, a mac and cheese burger with a bun covered in crushed cheese-flavored puffs, or the Muenster Smash Burger, which was served on a black bun with tater tots and covered in melted Muenster cheese and sriracha aioli.

But the star of this restaurant isn't the food; it's the entertainment! This out-of-this-world eatery features one of the biggest stars in the galaxy: Sonny Eclipse! Sonny is a singer, comedian, and astro-organist from Yew Nork City on the planet Zork. While Sonny's act was touring on Mars, his backup singers never arrived to perform their set. As Sonny was about to pack up the act, three beautiful voices began to sing out of the blue, joining Sonny in harmony and filling in as his backup singers. Named Space Angels, they cannot be seen (only heard), and they have been singing with Sonny ever since! Stop by Starlight Lounge inside Cosmic Ray's to catch Sonny Eclipse.

Park Pointer

★

Tomorrowland is the place to find characters that come from other planets, like the mischievous Experiment 626 (better known as Stitch)! One of the most beloved characters in Disney animation, Stitch is ready to meet you and your 'ohana. Stitch doesn't have a regular meeting spot in Tomorrowland currently, but he can often be found roaming around the land, posing for pictures, sneaking up on unsuspecting grandparents, or bugging the popcorn cart Cast Members for a snack! During the peak holiday season, Stitch may have a designated meet-and-greet spot. Check the My Disney Experience app for exact times and locations. Some other characters have been known to make an appearance around Tomorrowland, like Buzz Lightyear and Chip and Dale (in their spacesuits, of course). These character interactions have not been as consistent in recent years, but keep an eye out, because you never know who might fly into town!

PEDAL TO THE METAL!

Tomorrowland Speedway is another opening day attraction that has withstood the test of time. A parkgoer favorite for multiple generations, the attraction opened in 1971 as Grand Prix Raceway. This attraction allows little ones to take the wheel of a gas-powered car and speed around the Tomorrowland track. Reaching a whopping speed of 7 miles per hour, this is a family-friendly attraction where you can race against your family and into victory lane!

The original track was 3,100 feet in length and wrapped around a good portion of Tomorrowland—largely due to the fact that it was one of only two rides in the area! Over the years, the track has been shortened as neighboring attractions have been added. The first shortening occurred when Space Mountain was added, the second when Mickey's Birthdayland was added. It was shortened again for the relocation of Dumbo the Flying Elephant and was most recently shortened for TRON Lightcycle / Run. After all this, the track is now 30 percent smaller than it was in 1971 and stretches only 2,100 feet in length. Even with the shorter track, this is still a great attraction for little ones to have their first driving experience!

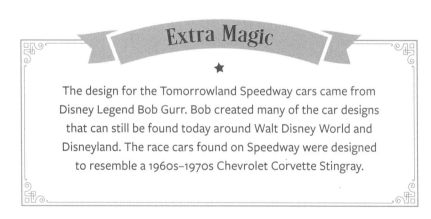

Extra Magic

★

The design for the Tomorrowland Speedway cars came from Disney Legend Bob Gurr. Bob created many of the car designs that can still be found today around Walt Disney World and Disneyland. The race cars found on Speedway were designed to resemble a 1960s–1970s Chevrolet Corvette Stingray.

YES, THERE IS COFFEE IN THE WORLD OF TOMORROW!

While you'll see many families carrying cups with the green Starbucks logo throughout Disney property, you can find another prevalent coffee option here too! Joffrey's Coffee has become the signature Disney coffee roaster, with a kiosk (or two) in each of the Florida Disney parks and both water parks, and it is provided in-room at most resorts on property. The company is based in Tampa, Florida, and also provides non-coffee options at most kiosks, like chai tea, iced teas, and sometimes smoothies. Seasonal mixed drinks can also be found at Joffrey's Coffee & Tea Company (sometimes even before the Starbucks drinks drop)! In Magic Kingdom, the only Joffrey's is located in the heart of Tomorrowland, just past The Lunching Pad and before the entrance of Space Mountain.

ICE CREAM THAT WILL LIFT YOU OFF YOUR FEET

Auntie Gravity's Galactic Goodies is well-known on this side of the galaxy for its soft serve ice cream. Serving up some delectable treats like Asteroid Shakes, Brownie Sundaes, and Cold Brew Floats, this is also the location that will test out specialty holiday soft serve items. Previous offerings have included the candy corn–flavored ice cream cone and sundaes served during the Halloween season. The seating area attached to this counter-service location has posters on the walls referencing the Tomorrowland attractions of today and yesterday. Most notable is the poster referencing The Timekeeper attraction located in Tomorrowland from 1994–2006. The attraction was voiced by actor Robin Williams.

Across from Auntie Gravity's is a little white-and-teal building that serves as an information stand for the Disney Vacation Club. This location is actually the remnants of one of the last ticketing booths that were scattered across Magic Kingdom from 1971–1982. Before the opening of EPCOT, Magic Kingdom utilized a similar ticketing system to that of Disneyland. Guests would pay per ride, and if they wanted to re-ride or go on a different ride within the categories listed in Chapter 1, they would have to go back and purchase additional tickets from a ticketing booth. After the ticketing system changed, most of the ticketing booths were removed, and very few can still be seen. This piece of Disney history is hiding in plain sight in Tomorrowland!

❓ A TIMEKEEPER AND A . . .

While you may remember Robin Williams as the host of The Timekeeper attraction in Tomorrowland, the actor also famously lent his voice to another beloved character from an animated Disney film.

Which Disney character was voiced by Robin Williams?

★

Did you know that Space Mountain has hosted real-life astronauts? In 1975, just three months after Space Mountain officially opened, the Apollo-Soyuz Test Project team took a break from NASA's Kennedy Space Center to visit Magic Kingdom. Apollo-Soyuz was unprecedented as it represented the first time the United States and the Soviet Union crewed a mission together. It was doubly impressive since it brought American astronauts and Soviet cosmonauts together during the Cold War! The research and data collected from this mission eventually helped build the International Space Station. It's funny to think that during their time preparing for their mission, the astronauts enjoyed a day at Magic Kingdom. There is even a photo of American astronaut Thomas Stafford shaking hands with Mickey in front of Space Mountain!

LAUNCH INTO ORBIT

Have you ever wanted to blast into space in your very own rocket? The Astro Orbiter attraction is the next-best thing! Ride an elevator to the upper deck above the Tomorrowland Transit Authority PeopleMover attraction to the boarding area. Once there, you are loaded into your rocket and take flight high above Tomorrowland. This ride operates very similarly to the Dumbo the Flying Elephant attraction; however, it is more intense, as you will complete eleven rotations per minute. That's one rotation every six seconds! The height and tilting sensations of the rockets make this ride seem even faster—especially in the evening.

If you were to add up the number of rotations that this attraction completes in a single year, you would travel a distance of over 1 million miles, which is equivalent to circling Earth forty-eight times. That's a lot of space travel!

TAKE ME TO YOUR REFRESHMENTS!

Near the middle of Tomorrowland is a red spaceship perched on top of a snack stand. Not only is this a great visual landmark, but it also provides snacks with a refreshing twist! While you can find the standard fare of popcorn, ice cream, and cold drinks here, the reason most guests come is for the refreshing feeling of walking through the misters installed underneath the spaceship! This feature lends the stand its name: Cool Ship! This spot is a great way to take a minute to recuperate from the sweltering Florida heat.

MOVE IT, PEOPLE!

One of the most popular attractions among Magic Kingdom and Disney fans is Tomorrowland Transit Authority PeopleMover—more commonly known and referred to simply as PeopleMover. Most guests love the novelty of how this attraction allows them to take in the sights of Tomorrowland as they travel around the area, even getting glimpses into the inside of other attractions, like Buzz Lightyear's Space Ranger Spin and Space Mountain. Other guests may just like the chance to prop their feet up for the ten-minute ride. Whatever you enjoy most about the ride, you might be surprised to learn that this unassuming transit system has a complete backstory!

The PeopleMover that guests ride on makes up just one of the three different transit lines within the Tomorrowland Transit Authority (Blue Line, Red Line, and Green Line). On the ride, you take a trip on the "intracity" Blue Line. While the Red and Green lines are not technically seen in the attraction, there is a reference to both transit lines on PeopleMover. During the ride, just before passing by the Star Traders shop, you'll see two robots. One is wearing a hat and holding what seem to be a briefcase and a newspaper. This scene represents the Red and Green Line transfer station. Space travelers can use the Red Line to journey off-planet across the galactic highway to other planets. Meanwhile, the Green Line takes Tomorrowland locals outside the city to the residential areas known as hover-burbs.

YOUR GUIDE TO TOMORROW (AND YESTERDAY)

While cruising through Tomorrowland on the Blue Line, your trip will be overseen by the ORAC-5 Commuter Computer that acts as the narrator for your journey. ORAC-5 is the fifth major update to the PeopleMover narration (hence the "5"), and the computer makes references to the original narrator (ORAC-1) and other attractions from Tomorrowland's past.

Here are some quotes from the narration of ORAC-5 on People-Mover that reference some of Tomorrowland's past attractions:

★ While passing the Monsters, Inc. Laugh Floor, ORAC-5 says, "Whether you have one eye or nine, take the time to see this show!" This is a reference to The Timekeeper attraction that was housed in the same building and featured a sassy robot assistant to The Timekeeper named 9-Eye.

★ Toward the end of the attraction, ORAC-5 says, "This is my favorite part because now is the time, now is the best time to go out and explore tomorrow today!" This references the lyrics of the Sherman brothers' song "The Best Time of Your Life," which was the former main attraction song of Carousel of Progress from 1975–1994 after it moved from California to Florida.

❓ WHAT MOVES THE MOVER?

Disney is famous for the different forms of ride technology it uses in its attractions. While many attractions share ride system technology with other attractions on Disney property, Tomorrowland Transit Authority PeopleMover uses a unique system that is not found anywhere else in Magic Kingdom! Attractions similar in style to PeopleMover often use Omnimover technology, which essentially means that individual ride cars sit atop a moving track that is often hidden for thematic purposes. PeopleMover, however, relies on a different type of ride motor technology to move its cars—it uses a series of electric currents to create a magnetic field. Opposing magnetic fields in the cars and the track propel the ride forward.

Can you guess what this system that moves PeopleMover is called?

    A. Linear induction motors

    B. A hidden chain system

    C. Solar-powered electric motors

As you pass through Tomorrowland, you may have noticed some metallic palm trees near the front of Space Mountain and toward the walkway of TRON Lightcycle / Run. The trees are called Power Palms. These seemingly random details actually have an interesting thematic story. Imagineers envisioned the palms acting as a futuristic power source that would be available in the world of tomorrow. Power Palms collect energy through their palm fronds and then store that energy in the coconut-like globes that hang from the trees. The "coconuts" would be collected by the Tomorrowland Power Company as a way to power Rocket Tower Plaza. If you look closely at the palms, you will notice that one of them is folded up slightly and the coconuts are missing, signifying that the energy has been collected from that tree by the Tomorrowland Power Company. While the palms are not functional, this is an amazing Imagineered idea for creatively collecting the power of tomorrow!

OUT-OF-THIS-WORLD HOT DOGS

A little-known fact about Tomorrowland is that the center of the land is known as Rocket Tower Plaza. This area consists of a stage area as well as the area around the entrance to PeopleMover and Astro Orbiter. In the theme for Tomorrowland, Rocket Tower Plaza is the center of the varying modes of transportation throughout the galaxy. The one thing that every transport hub needs is a good snack joint. Rocket

Tower Plaza is no exception and features The Lunching Pad! Located just below the ramps taking you up toward PeopleMover, this quick-service kiosk has an ample seating area and serves up some of the most creative all-beef hot dogs. Try a Jalapeño-Popper Dog with sriracha cream cheese, crispy onion straws, bacon, and spicy relish! There is also a Queso Fundido Hot Dog complete with street-corn relish and spiced tortilla strips. These hot dog options may vary as the Disney chefs try out new combinations, so make sure to check the My Disney Experience app to see what's cooking on this side of the galaxy!

JOIN BUZZ ON A CELESTIAL MISSION

Buzz Lightyear needs you to join him on an important mission to save the galaxy! The evil Emperor Zurg is once again up to his dastardly tricks, and you must launch a daring mission to stop him from stealing . . . AA batteries? Yes! Although Buzz calls the batteries in the attraction crystallic fusion cells, the design resembles the shape of an AA battery since guests have been transported to the world of toys after entering the ride. The same AA batteries were referred to as crystallic fusion cells in the *Buzz Lightyear of Star Command* cartoon series that ran from 2000–2001.

In Buzz Lightyear's Space Ranger Spin, you are tasked to join Buzz and little green aliens on a mission to stop Zurg and his alien robot army. Some of the aliens and robots also resemble toys, such as the windup dinosaur toys in the volcano scene and Rock 'Em Sock 'Em Robots in the robot attack scene. You hop aboard a ship and use laser cannons to fire the Zs spread throughout the attraction to gain points and stop Zurg. Can you become a Galactic Hero?

❓ TEST YOUR STAR COMMAND STATUS

Everyone loves a good competition, and Buzz Lightyear's Space Ranger Spin is a favorite place to try and beat your family and friends and get a high score! The Zs you try to hit with your laser cannons are scattered throughout the ride, and if you succeed, they award points based on the difficulty of their placement and a few other factors. After you finish racking up as many points as possible on the ride, you can see what Star Command rank you achieved!

Match the correct rank to the score ranges.

0–1,000	Planetary Pilot
1,001–10,000	Space Scout
10,001–100,000	Galactic Hero
100,001–300,000	Cosmic Commando
300,001–600,000	Ranger 1st Class
600,001–999,998	Star Cadet
999,999	Space Ace

JOKE MONSTER

The monster world needs your help! Set after the events of the hit Pixar film, Monsters, Inc. Laugh Floor welcomes humans into the monster world for a one-of-a-kind comedy show to collect laughs. Monstropolis now runs on "laugh power," which is known to be more powerful than screams. Mike Wazowski created this special comedy club to collect those laughs in a brand-new way. Mike is your "monster of ceremonies" and introduces three acts with original monsters that were created specifically for the attraction: Buddy Boil, Sam and Ella, and Marty Wazowski (who is Mike's nephew). Each monster has their own special running gags in the show and communicates with the audience.

While waiting in the queue, you can text some of your best jokes to the monster world for a chance to have your joke featured in the show! The phone number to text can be found on signage in the queue of the attraction.

Once inside, movable cameras can pick out members of the audience to find participants for the show. The monsters may ask you questions or invite you to help them perform a portion of their act. Just remember to laugh, because as Roz says, "The more you laugh, the more power we collect. The less you laugh—well, we may not have enough power to open the exit doors." So make some noise for your favorite monsters and enjoy the show!

Park Pointer

★

In recent years, a holiday overlay was added to Monsters, Inc. Laugh Floor featuring some holly jolly jokes. This overlay, however, is exclusive to guests that are attending a Mickey's Very Merry Christmas Party. The show is very cute and highly recommended. This is a great one to fit in at the beginning of the night before the festivities get into full swing.

On select nights starting in the end of August through December, the Magic Kingdom gets a little extra festive with special after-hour ticketed events. In the fall months, the park offers Mickey's Not-So-Scary Halloween Parties. These feature specialty food offerings, villainous meet-and-greet characters, frightful fun shows, the Mickey's Boo-To-You Halloween Parade, and, best of all, trick or treating throughout the park! After the spooky season is over, the park turns into a winter wonderland around the second week of November, ushering in Mickey's Very Merry Christmas Party. These parties are full of heartwarming shows, special character meet and greets in their most festive wear, Mickey's Once Upon a Christmastime Parade, and cookie stops around the park to get in a holly jolly mood. Since these after-hours events are set up a little differently than typical park admission, they can be less busy compared to a normal park day, making lines for rides shorter and more manageable. Check out the Disney website for more details to see if these parties might be a great addition to your plans!

🍴 A NIGHT TO REMEMBER IN TOMORROWLAND

Hidden in the farthest corner of Tomorrowland, just off the right side of Main Street U.S.A., is Tomorrowland Terrace Restaurant. This restaurant originally opened as a much-needed quick-service reinforcement for Magic Kingdom in the early 1970s. However, it has since become the location for Magic Kingdom's Fireworks Dessert Parties—it does not serve food at any other time of the day. These parties are not included with general admission pricing and must be purchased separately. Fireworks Dessert Parties are available most nights and are still available during holiday party events like Mickey's Not-So-Scary Halloween Party and Mickey's Very Merry Christmas Party. Check-in for your dessert party begins one hour prior to the fireworks show. Once inside the restaurant, an offering of all-you-care-to-enjoy desserts is available, such as chocolate silk tarts, chocolate-dipped strawberries, and other pastries prepared by Disney's chefs. The food options also include a variety of savory snacks such as cheeses and crackers. For guests over the age of twenty-one, an assortment of alcoholic beverages is included with your ticket price. Shortly before the fireworks show begins, Cast Members will escort your party to a reserved fireworks viewing location in Plaza Garden in the Hub grass area. This ensures your party has a prime viewing location for the spectacular fireworks show!

 THE GRAND FINALE

After a full day at Magic Kingdom, how do you wrap up your night in style? With fireworks, of course! The fireworks display has come a long way since the first show debuted at Disney World on October 24, 1971. In the opening year of Magic Kingdom, the fireworks show only lasted around six minutes. Now, with an average run time of eighteen minutes and projection-mapped displays on Cinderella Castle and Main Street, Disney fireworks shows have become the gold standard for theme parks around the world. Projection mapping is the use of 3D technology to display video projections onto every corner of the castle perfectly. These projections can do so many things, even making it seem like the castle is coming to life! More than fireworks set to music, Disney's nighttime spectaculars use fireworks to emphasize moments in a story told through music. These shows are created to emotionally connect with the audience through the characters, films, and magic of Disney.

Since Magic Kingdom opened in 1971, there have only been four distinct fireworks shows:

* *Fantasy in the Sky* ran from 1971–2003. While the show did go through some major changes during its thirty-two-year run, it remained more or less the same.
* *Wishes: A Magical Gathering of Disney Dreams* replaced *Fantasy in the Sky* in 2003 and ran through 2017.
* *Happily Ever After* appeared from 2017–2021.
* *Disney Enchantment* replaced *Happily Ever After* in 2021 and ran until 2023 to celebrate Disney World's fiftieth anniversary.
* *Happily Ever After* returned to Magic Kingdom in 2023 with some major updates to its projection technology but still maintained the same story and songs from the earlier version.

The Disney nighttime spectacular at Magic Kingdom is not to be missed and will almost certainly leave you feeling inspired, excited, and maybe a little emotional as well!

Creating Your Happily Ever After

We have just about finished up our grand tour of Magic Kingdom! You might be surprised to learn that knowing the best way to *leave* the park is just as important as knowing the best way to enter it. Here are a few suggestions: First decide when you actually want to leave the park. Many, *many* people will make the mistake of trying to leave immediately after the fireworks show. If you choose to do this, you and 53,000 other parkgoers will all be heading toward the Transportation and Ticketing Center at the same time. The lines for all forms of transportation leaving the park are long, kids and adults are "hangry" or exhausted, and joining the madness just isn't worth it unless you really need to leave then.

If you can, instead take some time to slowly make your way out of Magic Kingdom. Is there one more ride you want to try to get on before the park closes? Fantasyland is a great option to enjoy a few more attractions before heading out. You could also head over to Adventureland or Frontierland to try and get on Big Thunder Mountain Railroad one more time or catch the last sailing of Jungle Cruise for the evening.

Grabbing a snack before heading out can be a great choice as well! Casey's Corner and Cosmic Ray's are both open until about thirty minutes before the park closes, making them perfect last-minute spots to fuel up before heading out. You'll be enjoying your late-night French fries or corn dogs instead of waiting in line for transportation hungry and tired. This also gives the crowds a chance to head out of the park ahead of you, and the line for whatever form of transportation you need will be shorter as well. The stores on Main Street also typically stay open for about one hour after the park closes, and this can be a great time to pop in to snag that souvenir you have been thinking about all day or a bag of cotton candy for the road. (Note: There are some exceptions to regular operating hours—for example, if there are special holiday events happening—so check the My Disney Experience app for the latest information.)

One of the most incredible design elements of Main Street can also play a big role in your feelings as you exit the park. In Chapter 2, you learned that Main Street uses an Imagineering technique called forced perspective to make the buildings appear bigger than they actually are as you head down Main Street toward Cinderella Castle. This same technique functions in reverse as you leave the park—buildings start to feel smaller as you get farther from the castle. You may not realize it at first, but this can actually make you feel a bit melancholy as you exit the park! The castle and all the magic around it start to fade and seem incredibly far away, like the closing of a magical storybook. The same Main Street that once welcomed you to Magic Kingdom and pulled you in is now acting as a funnel out of the park. Your brain is picking up on all these tiny details, hence the melancholy. Some are more affected by this feeling than others, but don't be surprised if a tear comes to your eye out of nowhere when leaving!

Don't worry, Magic Kingdom isn't going anywhere anytime soon. Though it might change over the years, the gates of Magic Kingdom are always ready to welcome you and transport you to the most magical place on Earth. In the words of Mickey Mouse, "See ya real soon!"

Answers

INTRODUCTION

★ Which famous actor applied to be a Jungle Cruise Skipper and did not get the job—Josh Gad, Jim Gaffigan, or Terry Crews?

Answer: Josh Gad.

CHAPTER 2

★ True or False: Disney's patented aromatic system is called a Smellitizer.

Answer: True! These smell-emitting machines are known as Smellitizers.

★ What were Mickey's first words?

A. "Oh, boy!"

B. "Hiya, pal!"

C. "Hot dogs! Hot dogs!"

Answer: C., "Hot dogs! Hot dogs!"—which later led to Mickey's iconic catchphrase, "Hot dog!"

* While most of Main Street's services are no longer operational, which one is still functional—and features an authentic, turn-of-the-twentieth-century piece of equipment?

   A. Firehouse

   B. Mail service

   C. Dry cleaners

   Answer: B., Mail service. There is a functional Victorian-era postbox outside City Hall. (You can add some extra pixie dust to your snail mail by taking your letter or postcard into City Hall first and kindly asking a Cast Member to stamp it with the Main Street postal stamp.)

* Which candy bar was named after the horse?

   A. Milky Way

   B. Snickers

   C. Twix

   Answer: B., Snickers. Snickers candy bars were named after Snickers, the award-winning Mars family racehorse.

* There is one small detail in the statue that is important: Is Roy's hand above or below Minnie's hand?

   Answer: Below! Roy's hand is intentionally placed supporting Minnie's as a symbol of Roy's continued support of Walt through the years.

* Where else can you see Joe Potter mentioned?

   A. Street sign on Main Street

   B. Jungle Cruise life ring

   C. Ferryboat on Seven Seas Lagoon

Answer: C., Ferryboat on Seven Seas Lagoon. You might have even taken a ride on this ferryboat across Seven Seas Lagoon from the Transportation and Ticketing Center. The *General Joe Potter* ferryboat was rechristened in 1997 in honor of the man who helped build Magic Kingdom. Bonus fact: The other two ferryboats on Seven Seas Lagoon are named after Richard F. Irvine and Admiral Joe Fowler, two other Disney Legends that were key in the creation of Walt Disney World.

★ **What do the glasshouse Mickey balloons on Main Street and the confetti that falls during the Times Square Ball Drop in New York City have in common?**

A. Both concepts were designed by the same person.

B. Both items are made in New York City.

C. Both debuted at the Times Square Ball Drop in New York City.

Answer: A., Both concepts were designed by the same person. Treb Heining also worked with New York City to find ways to make the New Year's Eve ball drop more exciting. He ended up designing the "confetti blizzard" that has remained a tradition every year since 1992.

★ **Which holiday celebration was the first to make Disney World reach max capacity?**

A. Thanksgiving/Black Friday

B. Fourth of July

C. Christmas

D. Halloween

Answer: A., Thanksgiving/Black Friday (the weekend of 1971).

CHAPTER 3

★ True or False: "Fake Disney tree" is the correct translation for the Latin name *Disneyodendron eximus*.

Answer: False. The Latin name translates to "out-of-the-ordinary Disney tree."

★ Can you guess how many stairs there are on the way to the top of the treehouse?

A. 52

B. 98

C. 116

D. 134

Answer: C., 116.

★ What year did Dole Whip debut in Magic Kingdom?

A. 1971

B. 1984

C. 1986

D. 2010

Answer: B., 1984.

★ Which famous actor applied to be a Jungle Cruise Skipper and did not get the job?

A. Josh Gad

B. Jim Gaffigan

C. Terry Crews

Answer: A., Josh Gad

★ Do you know where to find the fez collection? Choose the correct option:

   A. The library

   B. The front door

   C. The bathrooms

   Answer: A., The library.

★ True or False: The original voice actor of Aladdin also is the same voice actor for the safety reminders on The Magic Carpets of Aladdin.

   Answer: True!

★ What is Citrikua the god of in Polynesian mythology?

   A. Rain

   B. Fire

   C. Pineapples

   D. None of the above

   Answer: D., None of the above. Citrikua was a tiki god created by Walt Disney Imagineering and does not appear in any real Polynesian mythology. According to Disney legend, Citrikua is the god of health, because citrus fruits are good for your health and are a great source of vitamin C!

* Do you know what Walt wanted Enchanted Tiki Room to be originally?

    A. A Polynesian dance show

    B. A water ride through the islands of Hawaii

    C. A Polynesian restaurant

    D. A thunderstorm-themed rollercoaster

    Answer: C., A Polynesian restaurant. In the original plans for the restaurant, the animatronic birds were to sing above the guests as they dined.

* Paul Frees's voice is also featured in a different attraction at Magic Kingdom. Can you guess which one?

    A. Big Thunder Mountain Railroad

    B. Haunted Mansion

    C. Walt Disney's Enchanted Tiki Room

    Answer: B., Haunted Mansion. He voices the disembodied Ghost Host!

CHAPTER 4

* What is the max speed you reach as you plummet down that last hill in Tiana's Bayou Adventure?

    A. 30 mph

    B. 60 mph

    C. 40 mph

Answer: The answer is C., 40 mph! You reach that max speed as you come barreling down the 45-degree-angle drop.

★ Throughout the restaurant, many items have inscriptions denoting who they belong to. Can you match the folklore item to the hero?

Paul Bunyan	Coonskin Cap
Lone Ranger	Tin Pot Hat
Casey Jones	Engineer Equipment
Buffalo Bill	Axe
Johnny Appleseed	Mask and Silver Bullet
Davy Crockett	Show Boots

Answer: Paul Bunyan: Axe; Lone Ranger: Mask and Silver Bullet; Casey Jones: Engineer Equipment; Buffalo Bill: Show Boots; Johnny Appleseed: Tin Pot Hat; Davy Crockett: Coonskin Cap.

★ Which is not one of the Big Thunder Mountain Railroad train names?

A. U.B. Bold

B. U.B. Strong

C. U.R. Courageous

D. U.R. Daring

E. I.M. Brave

F. I.M. Fearless

G. I.B. Hearty

Answer: B., U.B. Strong.

★ **Which coaster is the longest measured by ride time?**

A. TRON Lightcycle / Run

B. Seven Dwarfs Mine Train

C. The Barnstormer

D. Big Thunder Mountain Railroad

E. Space Mountain

Answer: D., Big Thunder Mountain Railroad. The out-of-control railroad has the longest ride duration out of all five coasters in the park, with a ride time of three minutes and twenty-six seconds.

CHAPTER 5

★ **Which president was the first to record their speaking part for The Hall of Presidents?**

A. George Washington

B. Abraham Lincoln

C. Joe Biden

D. Bill Clinton

Answer: D., Bill Clinton.

★ **True or False: The bell in Walt Disney World is visited more than the original Liberty Bell in Philadelphia.**

Answer: True. The Philadelphia Liberty Bell sees an average of 1 million guests each year, but the bell in Magic Kingdom gets over 17 million.

★ **Which full-length Disney feature film followed *The Adventures of Ichabod and Mr. Toad* and became a big commercial success?**

Answer: *Cinderella* (1950).

★ **Which area was added to the Haunted Mansion?**

Answer: The Endless Staircase area. This addition took inspiration from M.C. Escher's art piece *Relativity* and the Winchester Mystery House in California with its stairways to nowhere.

CHAPTER 6

★ **Why is the line always long for Peter Pan's Flight?**

A. It's so popular.

B. The attraction moves slowly.

C. It has a low ride capacity.

Answer: C., It has a low ride capacity. Due to the suspended ride system, each pirate ship only has a capacity of about two adults or one adult and two children, which allows for just roughly eight hundred guests per hour on average. For comparison, Pirates of the Caribbean has one of the largest capacities in Magic Kingdom and can handle an average of 2,600 guests per hour.

★ In the film, Peter gives the Darling children very specific instructions for how to find Never Land—can you remember them? How do you find Never Land in the night sky?

A. "First star to the right, until you find the light."

B. "Second star to the left, and straight on till evening."

C. "Second star to the right, and straight on till morning."

Answer: C., "Second star to the right, and straight on till morning."

★ What color cat is Figaro?

A. Black and white

B. Brown

C. White

Answer: A., Black and white.

★ How many horses are on Prince Charming Regal Carrousel?

A. 80

B. 65

C. 90

Answer: C., 90. The original Liberty Carrousel had eighty horses before coming to Walt Disney World, where the additional horses were added and a handful of sleighs were removed.

★ Can you match which character is associated with these award years?

CHARACTER	YEARS OF SERVICE
Pluto	20
Tinker Bell	10
Simba	5
TaDa Mickey	25

Answer: Pluto: 5, TaDa Mickey: 10, Simba: 20, and Tinker Bell: 25.

★ Match each statement to the correct answer:

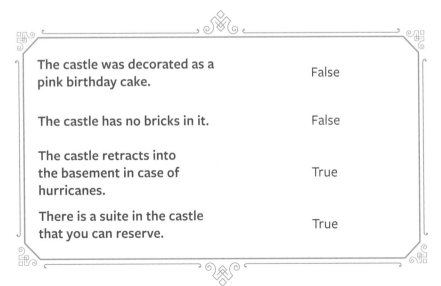

The castle was decorated as a pink birthday cake.	False
The castle has no bricks in it.	False
The castle retracts into the basement in case of hurricanes.	True
There is a suite in the castle that you can reserve.	True

Answer: The castle was decorated as a pink birthday cake: true. The castle has no bricks in it: true. The castle retracts to the basement in case of hurricanes: false. There is a suite in the castle that you can reserve: false.

★ **How many pieces of Italian glass were used in creating the mosaics for Cinderella Castle?**

   A. 10,000

   B. 500,000

   C. 250,000

   D. Over 1 million

   Answer: D., Over 1 million. (That includes more than five hundred color variations.)

★ **What do the numbers on the train cars represent? (No, these are not the winning lottery numbers.)**

   Answer: These are in reference to the opening years of the four Walt Disney World theme parks—1971: Magic Kingdom, 1982: EPCOT, 1989: Disney's Hollywood Studios (as Disney-MGM Studios Theme Park), and 1998: Animal Kingdom.

CHAPTER 7

★ **Can you guess what max speed is reached on Space Mountain?**

   A. 28 mph

   B. 42 mph

   C. 60 mph

   Answer: A., 28 mph.

- ★ Which Disney character was voiced by Robin Williams?

  Answer: Genie from Disney's *Aladdin*.

- ★ Can you guess what this system that moves PeopleMover is called?

    A. Linear induction motors

    B. A hidden chain system

    C. Solar-powered electric motors

  Answer: A., Linear induction motors.

- ★ Match the correct rank to the score ranges.

0–1,000	Planetary Pilot
1,001–10,000	Space Scout
10,001–100,000	Galactic Hero
100,001–300,000	Cosmic Commando
300,001–600,000	Ranger 1st Class
600,001–999,998	Star Cadet
999,999	Space Ace

Answer:

0–1,000	Star Cadet
1,001–10,000	Space Scout
10,001–100,000	Ranger 1st Class
100,001–300,000	Planetary Pilot
300,001–600,000	Space Ace
600,001–999,998	Cosmic Commando
999,999	Galactic Hero

Index

Note: Page numbers in parentheses indicate intermittent references.
Page numbers in *italics* indicate answers to quizzes.

About the Authors

DANIELLE KELLY, known as The Dapper Danielle to her more than half a million social media followers, has exploded into an influential personality known for creating authentic and consistent Disney-themed content. A former Disney Cast Member with more than a decade of experience, Danielle uses her knowledge to illuminate the stories, people, and history that go into the most magical and happiest places on Earth. Between speaking engagements, podcast recordings, and content creation, Danielle is most likely to be at a Disney park obsessing over Orange Bird merch, planning her next fabulous outfit, and reminding everyone to: "Night night, sleep tight, dream of churros tonight!"

IAN WILSON was born in Tallahassee, Florida, and raised in Anchorage, Alaska. Living between two diametrically different places has helped Ian, as an editor, connect the abstract to the tangible, the artistic to the quantified, and the wild to the refined. Ian has been helping authors find the right words for their ideas for the last five years and has supported titles ranging from social commentary to works of fiction. He currently lives in Nashville, Tennessee, with his wife and new baby.

Bring the magic of Disney home!

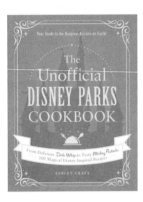

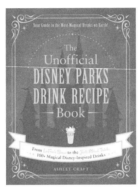

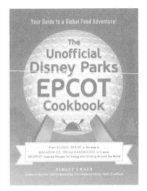

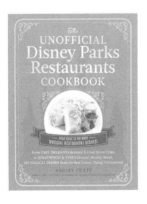

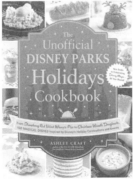

Pick up or download your copies today!